£12·00

Crucial Study Texts for Psychology Degree Courses

Titles in series

Clinical Psychology	ISBN: 1 903337 20 8	Price £12.00
Cognitive Psychology	ISBN: 1 903337 13 5	Price £12.00
Developmental Psychology	ISBN: 1 903337 14 3	Price £12.00
Introductory Psychology: History		
Themes and Perspectives	ISBN: 1 903337 17 8	Price £12.00
Research Methods and Statistics	ISBN: 1 903337 15 1	Price £9.99

To order, please call our order line 0845 230 9000, or email
orders@learningmatters.co.uk, or visit our website www.learningmatters.co.uk

Clinical Psychology

Andy Field

Psychology series editor:
Eamon Fulcher

First published in 2003 by Crucial, a division of Learning Matters Ltd.

British Library Cataloguing in Publication Data
A CIP record for this book is available from the British Library.

ISBN 1 903337 20 8

Cover design by Topics – The Creative Partnership
Project management by Deer Park Productions
Text design by Code 5 Design
Typeset by PDQ Typesetting, Newcastle under Lyme
Printed and bound by Bell & Bain Ltd, Glasgow

Learning Matters Ltd
33 Southernhay East
Exeter EX1 1NX
Tel: 01392 215560
Email: info@learningmatters.co.uk
www.learningmatters.co.uk

Contents

Acknowledgements..vii

Introduction: Studying clinical psychology at degree level..1

1 Classifying mental illness..9
   Chapter summary 9
   Assessment targets 9
   Section 1 Why do we classify? 9
   Section 2 How are mental disorders classified? 13
   Section 3 Assessing *DSM-IV* 16
   Section 4 End of chapter assessment..18
   Section 5 Further reading...18

2 Approaches to mental illness 19
   Chapter summary 19
   Assessment targets 19
   Section 1 Psychodynamic approaches..19
   Section 2 Behavioural models..22
   Section 3 Cognitive models..24
   Section 4 Biological models 26
   Section 5 End of chapter assessment..29
   Section 6 Further reading...29

3 Specific phobias 30
   Chapter summary 30
   Assessment targets 30
   Section 1 What is a specific phobia?..30
   Section 2 Do we learn to be scared? 32
   Section 3 Are we born to fear? 35
   Section 4 Do we think ourselves into being scared? 36
   Section 5 How are specific phobias treated? 37
   Section 6 End of chapter assessment..40
   Section 7 Further reading...40

4 Panic disorder and social phobia 41
   Chapter summary 41
   Assessment targets 41
   Section 1 How are social phobia and panic different? 41
   Section 2 Can we explain panic disorder?...44
   Section 3 Can we explain social phobia?...48
   Section 4 Can we treat panic disorder and social phobia? 50
   Section 5 End of chapter assessment..53
   Section 6 Further reading...54

5 Generalised anxiety disorder (GAD)..55
   Chapter summary 55

Assessment targets 55
Section 1 What is GAD? 55
Section 2 What is worry and why does it persist?..57
Section 3 Do we think ourselves into being anxious? 60
Section 4 Are we born anxious? 61
Section 5 How is GAD treated?..61
Section 6 End of chapter assessment...63
Section 7 Further reading...63

6   **Obsessive compulsive disorder (OCD)**..**64**
Chapter summary 64
Assessment targets 64
Section 1 What is obsessive compulsive disorder?..64
Section 2 Explanations of OCD..68
Section 3 How do we treat OCD?...71
Section 4 End of chapter assessment...72
Section 5 Further reading...72

7   **Eating disorders** **74**
Chapter summary 74
Assessment targets 74
Section 1 What are eating disorders? 74
Section 2 Can we explain eating disorders?...77
Section 3 How are eating disorders treated?..81
Section 4 End of chapter assessment...84
Section 5 Further reading...85

8   **Depression** **86**
Chapter summary 86
Assessment targets 86
Section 1 What is depression?..86
Section 2 Does depression come from thinking?..91
Section 3 Can we learn to be depressed? 93
Section 4 What's the role of serotonin in depression? 94
Section 5 How is depression treated? 96
Section 6 End of chapter assessment...98
Section 7 Further reading...98

9   **Schizophrenia**..**99**
Chapter summary 99
Assessment targets 99
Section 1 What is schizophrenia? 100
Section 2 Do our families make us schizophrenic?...103
Section 3 The role of the brain in schizophrenia...105
Section 4 Cognitive theories of schizophrenia..107
Section 5 How is schizophrenia treated?...109
Section 6 End of chapter assessment...111
Section 7 Further reading...111

References **112**

Index **123**

Acknowledgements

I've listened to Cradle of Filth, Muse, Foo Fighters, Tom Waits, Queens of the Stone Age, Mark Lanegan, The Get Up Kids, Frank Black, Hundred Reasons and Godspeed You Black Emperor while writing this book.

Thanks to Cathy Creswell and Ele Jones, who are clinical psychologists, for providing me with the crucial case studies for eating disorders and obsessive compulsive disorder (OCD) (Ele) and generalised anxiety disorder (GAD), panic and depression (Cathy). I'm really grateful for them frequently taking time out of their busy schedules to talk to me about clinical psychology. I am also grateful (although he might be surprised to know it) to Charles Legg who taught me psychobiology when I was an undergraduate. Much of the schizophrenia chapter stems from his excellent tuition and his ability to make me fascinated by his course.

Finally, I am grateful to Mandy Preece, Joanne Lawson and an anonymous reviewer who provided detailed editorial advice or comments that vastly improved the final version of this text.

Dedication

This book is dedicated to Leonora.

Introduction
Studying clinical psychology at degree level

In this introduction we will look at some of the different methods of assessment that you are likely to encounter, and I'll try to give you a bit of advice about two of the main forms of assessment: exams and essay writing.

In this section I'll say a few things about how to use this book and how clinical psychology is likely to be assessed.

What should I use this book for?

Obviously the material I cover may not be the same as in your particular clinical course, but what I want to do is at least give you some ideas of the diagnosis, major theories and treatment of different disorders. Regardless of your specific course, this will be good background reading.

It's not an exhaustive text, but it should give you the main pointers and, if you've bunked off all your lectures and realise you have an exam tomorrow, I'd hope that a bit of selective cramming from here would enable you to pass your exam.

General study tips

Taking responsibility

Unlike at A level, studying at degree level requires a lot of initiative. You won't be spoon-fed nearly as much, and will often be expected to find your own reading materials and manage your study time. So you have to motivate yourself, and use your own initiative and self-discipline rather than relying on constant supervision. Lecturers love hard-working students, but we won't get particularly annoyed with you if you don't work hard because people have to make their own decisions in life: we realise that some people want to work hard and get a good grade, while others want more of a mix of work and life experience from their degree and are not as fussed about the grade they get. I think it's fair to say that the more you put into your degree the more you'll get out. I doubt there is a lecturer in the country who isn't absolutely delighted when someone comes to them and says 'I've done all the reading, but there's just something I still don't understand.' However, it is equally as soul destroying for us if, after we've put our heart and soul into teaching you, someone turns up and says 'I haven't been to any of your lectures, I don't have the course handout, could you just spend an hour telling me what you've covered and what I should write in my exam.'

Although it's probably a scary thought to be responsible for how well you do, you shouldn't worry because this was always true in the past. Your school or college grades were down to your hard work (or lack of), during these periods, you just had a bit more specific guidance. However, don't worry because people will help you if you're stuck or feeling stressed.

Managing your time

If you actually knew me personally you would realise how laughable this section is: I am already late for my deadline to submit this book manuscript, and I haven't actually stuck to a deadline since I finished my degree! However, this should but reassure you that everyone finds time management hard (even your lecturers!).

Most people are surprised by how much 'free time' they have at university. You'll probably only spend, at most, ten to 20 hours of the week in lectures or seminars. The remaining time is for 'independent study'. Some people will decide to 'independently study' the effects of alcohol on thoughts and behaviours, or 'independently study' how many women (or men) they can pull. I couldn't possibly recommend any of these activities (what with being an upstanding member of society and all that), but I should point out that the remaining 20-30 hours of the week are supposed to be time in which you study. However, fear not, this still leaves you plenty of time to sleep and get up to mischief.

It's true that you will need to work pretty hard to get a decent degree, but because you don't want to miss out entirely on the fun things in life it's a good idea to manage your work time efficiently. If you spend all your time working and no time getting up to mischief then you'll end up like me, and trust me, you really don't want that to happen.

At university, deadlines are strict (at the University of Sussex, for example, only medical evidence is accepted as an excuse for late work). At the start of your course, you should be told the deadlines for work that you need to submit – often in a course handbook or maybe on an overhead in a lecture – and no one will chase you to meet this deadline. As I said, deadlines are strict, so give yourself time to finish and print the work. Remember that on deadline day there will be 100 others who haven't followed this advice all trying to print off essays five minutes before the deadline. Just to add to the misery computers have a tendency to respond to this excess demand by crashing and sending self-destruct signals to the printer! So, work well ahead of deadlines and back up any work you do (I, for example, have three back-ups of this book manuscript at any given moment!).

Do what you're told

I'll admit that lecturers differ hugely in the quantity of support they give you. Not just emotional support, but written support. Nevertheless, even the worst ones will have written things down, or told you things, that are important. These documents in the worst case tell you what to do and how often to do it (e.g. two essays of 2,000 words to be submitted on 7 November and 10 December respectively). At best, they tell you what to read, where to find that reading, general advice, a few jokes and where to get help if you need it. Read any instructions like this extremely carefully. If you just skim them and do not remember the details, you may end up not knowing what you're supposed to do. If lecturers have written something down, they can be quite unsympathetic to people who are in a mess simply because they couldn't be bothered to read it. I guess the motto is: before you go and ask something, just quickly check that the answer isn't already sitting in your bag.

Arranging to study

Some people study in groups and others study alone. Whatever you prefer, you need to plan where, when and how. It is very important to choose somewhere suitable to study. You need to find a place where you have some space and where you can concentrate. This might not be in the university library. If you work in groups, then try to schedule 'chat time' and 'work time' so that you don't spend all day talking about non-work-related topics. A few tips (according to Miles, 2001) are:

- avoid having to study when you are too tired to concentrate properly;
- select the studying times best suited to you;
- set yourself time targets for studying – you need to take breaks to remain fresh.

Learning from textbooks

In the first year you'll do most of your learning from textbooks (or course notes if you have obsessive lecturers like me who prepare lots of them and stick them on the web). In the second year you'll be expected to read articles in journals (see next section), and by the third year you really won't be using many textbooks at all if you want to impress your lecturers. You might buy a textbook on clinical and abnormal psychology or just rely on your library having copies.

If you do buy a book use it, deface it, and generally get your value for money. If you rely on library books then don't do any of these things, just read it without bending the spine too much! Books are there to be read, and publishers often produce them with large margins so you can scribble stuff on them to help you re-locate important things. If you're worried about not being able to re-sell the book when you don't need it, then write in pencil that can be erased!

One note about notes, though, is be selective – only highlight key things.

Using old books

If you have studied A level or AS level psychology, or psychology on an Access course, you may well have studied clinical psychology as part of that course and you may have textbooks that cover some of the topics you are covering in your degree. It's fine to use these books as background reading to remind yourself about a topic, but even in the first year most of the books you use are much more detailed than at A level. At degree level we expect you to step up a gear, so if you rely on your old book, you'll very soon start getting worse marks as everyone else's essays become more detailed and yours remain stuck at A level standard!

Journal articles

One way to impress your lecturers is to read journal articles. Journals are sort of like magazines (only considerably more boring) that publish collections of articles by psychologists around the world. These articles take two general forms:

- research papers (these are like your undergraduate laboratory reports and are where academics publish an experiment or a collection of experiments that investigate some scientific issue); and
- review papers (these are where academics summarise theories about a given scientific issue and experiments relating to those theories).

These journals publish on specific areas of life and this is usually self-evident from the title. So, the *Journal of Experimental Psychology: Learning, Memory and Cognition* publishes experimental papers about human learning, human memory and cognition in general. There are a few journals, however, that publish articles that cover a wide range of topics—for example, *Psychological Review* and *Psychological Bulletin* publish review papers and theoretical papers from every area of psychology.

Why are journals a good thing to read? They come out a few times a year and so they are a good way to keep up with state-of-the-art research. Textbooks are out of date almost as soon as they are published because new research and theories are being developed all of the time. Also, because you're looking at the original source (not someone else's summary of it) you can read all of the details and evaluate the evidence for yourself.

CRUCIAL TIP

When writing an essay look around your library for the latest editions of journals and see if there's any relevant new research. If you find any, and incorporate this into your essay, it looks really impressive and good marks are bound to follow! Given how impressed lecturers generally are with efforts to incorporate new evidence into essays it absolutely amazes me how many students don't look at recent journal articles.

Some useful journals for clinical psychology are (in my view):

- *American Journal of Psychiatry*
- *Archives of General Psychiatry*
- *Behavior Therapy*
- *Behaviour Research and Therapy*
- *British Journal of Clinical Psychology*
- *British Journal of Psychiatry*

- *Clinical Psychology Review* (only published review papers so is a good place to look for summaries of clinical issues)
- *Cognition and Emotion*
- *Cognitive Therapy and Research*
- *International Journal of Eating Disorders*
- *Journal of Anxiety Disorders*
- *Journal of Abnormal Psychology*
- *Journal of Consulting and Clinical Psychology*
- *Schizophrenia Research*
- *Schizophrenia Bulletin.*

Using books and journals

Most of this section is based on Jeremy Miles' (2001) *Crucial Study Guide to Research Methods and Statistics*. Reading books and (especially) journals can be boring. Essentially, as Jeremy points out, brains are lazy things; they don't want to expend lots of energy doing stuff. Partly this is because they have a lot to do: I mean they have to work out whether you need to eat, whether you remembered to lock the front door and feed the cat and so on. On top of all of this you then ask it to read a book. So it thinks to itself, 'Well, ok, I'll read the book, but only if I don't have to put too much effort in.' This is why we all get the experience where we're mid-way through a page and we suddenly realise that we haven't got a clue what we've been reading for the past ten minutes. This is basically your brain having a bit of a laugh, and switching itself off and seeing how long it will take you to notice. So your brain keeps the eyes scanning the page and then goes off and does something more important like thinking about how nice Hawaii is at this time of year. However, we can force our brain to keep working and not think about Hawaii. Jeremy suggests the **SQ3R technique**, which stands for:

- **Survey**: have a quick skim through the text to see what it is going to tell you. At this stage just have an overall look at the text to see what it is going to be about. You can do this by looking at the subheadings, figures or diagrams; reading the abstract (if there is one) and the introductory paragraph. If it's a journal article look at the subheadings and read the abstract, look at any tables or graphs, read the first paragraph of the introduction, and the first paragraph of the discussion, and maybe the last paragraph of the discussion.

- **Question**: take one section at a time. In a journal article the sections are likely to be the introduction, method, results and discussion. In a textbook the chapter will be divided up into main sections and subsections. Before you read each section, ask yourself four questions: what will this section tell me? Why did the author write this section? What will I learn from reading this section? How does this relate to what I already know?

- **Read**: the third stage is to actually read the thing. Read the section that you have asked yourself questions about and keep the questions in mind as you read (this will keep your brain awake). Don't try to read too much, stick to manageable amounts of information and don't make notes at this stage, because it will distract you from reading and understanding the text.

- **Recall**: one thing we know about memory is that it stores information better if once it has stored something it is forced to recall it. So now is the time to make notes by trying to recall the important parts of the section that you just read, and write them down. Don't just copy the text because your brain will take the opportunity to have a nap, so instead just write notes on what you can remember. If you've stuck with manageable chunks of reading you'll recall enough to make some notes. If you can't remember something, go and read it again but wait until you have finished reading before you start to make notes again.

- **Review**: finally, review what you have learned by testing yourself to make sure that you have remembered what you read. If you aren't sure, or can't remember some- thing, go back to your notes to check.

Writing essays

Clinical psychology will probably involve writing essays both for coursework and in exams. There are some general tips for essay writing on my departmental web site at *http://www.cogs.susx.ac.uk/psych/WriteThatEssay.html* (I'm conscious of how web addresses change so if that fails find the Sussex web site (*http://www.sussex.ac.uk*), which won't change, search for my web page and I'll have links to all of these things!) All I'm going to say is that essays are really quite easy to write if you stick to a few basic principles.

Answer the question

Everyone will tell you that the most common mistake in essay writing is that people don't answer the question. So they see a question like 'How effective are drug therapies for depression?' as an excuse to write as much as they know about depression. In fact, this sort of question doesn't require you to talk much about depression (other than a brief description of what depression is and what the biological model is). Instead, you need to talk mainly about how antidepressants are thought to work, evaluate (critically) the evidence for their success and then present an answer.

Back up your argument with evidence

This is very important. When you state a fact in your essay, you must cite evidence for it (usually a piece of research). We usually identify a piece of research by the standard method of giving the name of the author and the date it was published. For example, don't make sweeping statements that are not backed up by evidence like 'antidepressants don't seem to work because my mate takes them and she's still as miserable as sin.' Instead, try to stick to the evidence by looking to published research, and views of other writers. So, you could write 'Picciotto, MacKaye, Lally, & Canty (1994) found that patients taking 8mg of Prozac showed significant improvement in self-reported depression (using the Beck Depression Inventory) after one week and one month.' You might have difficulty getting used to this, but if you look at journal articles and book chapters, you will find that they are full of citations and this is the style for which you're aiming.

> ──────────── CRUCIAL TIP ────────────
>
> The previous point relates to statements of opinion, as well as statements of psychological fact. If, for example, you write, 'numerous studies have shown that taking antidepressants is beneficial for depressives' you must then either list the numerous studies to which you refer, or say who has made the claim. So you could say, 'Field (2003) claims that numerous studies have shown ...', or say 'numerous studies have shown that taking antidepressants is beneficial for depressives (MacKaye, 2002; Pfizer, 2001; Picciotto, MacKaye, Lally, & Canty, 1994, 1990).' The same is true for statements like 'most clinicians agree that '... or 'there has been little research to substantiate the claim that Prozac ...'.

Be critical

It is important not to take evidence at face value. So, if you spot something wrong in a study, then don't be afraid to say so. For example, you could say 'MacKaye (1994) found that patients taking 8mg of Prozac showed significant improvement in self-reported depression (using the Beck Depression Inventory) after one week and one month. However, ten of their patients dropped out of the study and so their data were excluded, and Critical and Pedantic (1996) have subsequently shown that the Beck Depression Inventory is prone to practice effects, whereby ratings improve over time anyway.'

Use recent evidence

As I mentioned earlier, use recent evidence. So, you could say 'Pedantic (2003) recently showed that when more sensitive measures are used, patients taking 8mg of Prozac showed no significant improvement in their depressed state.' Basically, you want your essay to stand out from those of other people. Everyone will be citing evidence from the set textbook, so if you can find some papers that others haven't used then your lecturer will know you've put in that extra bit of effort.

Essay structure

Another vital thing is that the essay must be **structured**. Essays just tell a story and so need to have a beginning, middle and an end. These take the form of an introduction, a main section and a conclusion.

- **Introduction**: this section doesn't need to be too long. You just need to lay out the main terms you're dealing with and give an overview of your essay. In most clinical psychology essays you will start them by discussion of the disorder about which you're writing. So you're always going to begin with a brief summary of how the disorder is diagnosed. In the example we've been using you could begin by saying 'Depression is characterised by excessively low mood and can be associated with sleep problems, the key diagnostic criteria are ....'

CRUCIAL TIP

Ending your introduction with a summary of what you're going to talk about is a good idea for two reasons:

- it makes you think about your structure before you write your essay; and
- it makes it obvious to the person reading the essay what your structure is (and this often creates an illusion that your essay is more structured than it might actually be because the reader knows what to expect).

- **Main body**: this is the vast majority of your essay. In this section you need to answer the question as it is set (you can't just write everything you know and then hope to tie it all up in the conclusion). A good model is to present a certain **model** or **idea**, then present the **evidence** for that model, and then any **contradictory evidence**. Remember that your main body has to have a logical flow. So, for our antidepressants example, you need to start by telling the reader how these drugs work (that is, the biological model of depression and how these drugs fit in with the model) and distinguish different types of antidepressant medication. You then critically present evidence that antidepressants work, and then critically present material that suggests that they don't work. Throughout this section you need to evaluate what you read (think back to 'be critical').

- **Conclusion**: this section is relatively short (but not as short as some students make it). Here you need to go over your evidence (don't present any new material) and reach a decision about whether there is better evidence that antidepressants do work, or that they don't. The position you take is irrelevant; all that's important is that you give a reason that is based on the evidence you've presented. However, the important phrase here is 'based on the evidence you've presented': it's all too common to see things like 'the evidence clearly suggests that antidepressants have limited efficacy; however, I take them and I feel much happier now so they must be effective.' The person who set the question didn't ask 'do antidepressants work for you?' He or she asked whether drug treatments are effective generally!

CRUCIAL TIP

You'd be amazed how many people write their essay and then just tag on a few lines as a conclusion. Don't do this! The conclusion should be where you thread the strands of your essay together into a coherent paragraph. So the conclusion should be a substantial paragraph.

Finally, learn how to punctuate – it will improve the flow of your essay (and most academics are pedantic and get irritated by poor punctuation!). Larry Trask has some good tips on the web: *http://www.cogs.susx.ac.uk/local/doc/punctuation/node00.html* and if that fails, then get hold of his book, *The Penguin Guide to Punctuation* (Trask, R. L., 1997) or a similar text.

Doing exams

This section looks at a few tips for doing exams.

Don't revise every topic

Different courses will have different types of exams: some will ask you to answer a few questions from a selection of many (for example, answer two questions from a choice of five), whereas other exams might combine essay questions with short questions (multiple choice, or short answers). In both cases, the only way to guarantee you can answer all questions on an exam paper is to revise every topic. However, in reality this isn't practical because it's too much for anyone's brain to cope with so you'll end up revising lots of topics but in too little depth. If your exam is just based on choosing essays from a selection, then it's much better to revise a few topics, but in a lot of detail – otherwise it's just a waste of effort. If your exam combines essays with short answer questions, then you will have to know a bit of everything, but even here you can revise a selection of topics in great detail (for the essays), and just learn the important information about the other topics (for the short answers).

The best way to pick your essay topics is to 'question guess', that is, take educated guesses at what topics are likely to come up. This isn't as hard as it sounds because most lecturers are fairly predictable (believe it or not most of us don't want to catch you out in exams). There are several things you can do:

- **Past papers**: most universities keep past exam papers (Sussex students, for example, can access them on the web or get them from the library). This will give you an idea of the types of questions your lecturer asks. If they've been there a few years this will also give you a good idea of what topics they tend to ask about. However, if your lecturer is new then this isn't helpful because they won't have set the past papers!

- **Pet topics**: think about your lecturer's 'pet' topics or the time spent on a topic in the course. So for example, if I give two lectures on schizophrenia and only one on everything else, then it's a fair guess that schizophrenia will come up in some form or another.

- **Ask your lecturer**: Some lecturers (like me) are quite transparent about what topics will come up. Although it's unreasonable to ask them what questions they've set, I don't think it's unreasonable to ask them what topics are coming up.

When you've picked likely topics, do extra reading on them; consider the key issues that have been raised (again the lectures are good places to work out what the lecturer thinks are the key issues). Like with coursework, to get first class marks you need a well-argued essay that draws on a variety of sources and recent evidence.

Revision

One of my undergraduate lecturers, Charles Legg, gave our year some very good advice before my finals: **do your thinking before the exam**. Brains don't work very well when they're stressed, so it's very difficult to think up good, well-structured essay answers in the exam. Therefore, try to think about likely questions and how you'd answer them before you enter the exam.

The way I adapted this advice was to generate some very general questions, for example 'what is the biological basis of schizophrenia?', answer them and then learn them by heart. A question like this gives you lots of stock information that can be slotted into other essays such as 'what is the role of enlarged ventricles in the development of schizophrenia?' So you could learn a paragraph describing the diagnostic criteria of a disorder (that will always be handy), rote-learn paragraphs describing important models, and so on. If you rote-learn paragraphs then all you need to do is to recite the relevant bits of model answers in the exam, or more precisely, combine segments of different model answers to answer the questions as set. So if you decide to revise obsessive-compulsive disorder (OCD), for example, then you could write an essay on symptoms, one on theories and one on treatment. That way you could adapt any one of these or combine bits of them to answer virtually any question on OCD.

That's all very well, but how do you learn them? Psychology students are lucky in that they study memory and learning and so we can use the tricks of the trade to help learn things. First, we can use what we know about memory:

- **Spaced retrieval/rehearsal is better than cramming**: if you learnt something now, and then tried to retrieve it an hour later, and then a day later, and then a week later and then a month later, you'd probably remember it for life. Spaced rehearsal/retrieval is the best way to learn, so try to retrieve information that you've learnt. For example, you could try reading your term essays once a week, or even once a month, and that will give you a good base on which to build.

- **Use mnemonics to remember lists of things**: for example, the characteristic symptoms in schizophrenia are: Delusions, Disorganized speech, Catatonic behaviour, Hallucinations, Negative symptoms. You remember the first letters of these symptoms (**DDCHN**) using a phrase that has the same letters. Sometimes you can use something that conveys a useful fact. In this case, you might use **D**rugs **D**on't **C**ure **H**er **N**egative symptoms and, in fact, antipsychotic drugs don't address negative symptoms (see Chapter 9).

- **Imagery**: if you can imagine anything wild or bizarre associated with bits of information then they will stick in your memory.

- **Mapping**: some people devise routes and place bits of information at each stop on a route. So, if you think about your route to campus, then mentally place bits of information along your route. This creates an association network of information that's mapped to daily activities.

CRUCIAL TIP

Another lecturer when I was an undergraduate, Graham Davey, who is an expert on learning, also imparted some very useful advice to my year: reinforce interest in your work. People tend to work and revise until they're really bored and then go and make some tea and have a break ('I'm bored so I'll go and have some chocolate'). All this does is reward you for being unmotivated! What you should do instead is reinforce positive motivational states. That is, when you're actually quite interested in what you're doing take a break *then* and do something nice. That way you'll reinforce hard work, rather than reinforcing boredom!

In the exam
My final tips for the exam itself are:

- **Stick to time**: give yourself equal time to answer each question and stick rigidly to these times. It's easier to get the first 50% of marks on a question than it is to pick up an extra 10% at the top end of the scale. So, if you've answered a question and run out of time, you'll earn more marks by spending ten minutes starting the next question than you will spending those 10 minutes trying to push your mark from a 65% to a 75% on the current question.

- **Answer the question that you can most easily answer first**: this will calm you down! However, still spend the allocated time on it: don't take longer because it's your best question! If you're running low on time you can always leave a page or two blank and come back to the question if you have time at the end.

- **Answer the question as set**: don't just write everything you know on the topic. You can't write a lot in an exam so stay focused on what the question actually asks!

- **Write a brief structure first**: don't spend too long on this (a few minutes at most), but it does help make sure that your answer is logical.

Chapter 1
Classifying mental illness

Chapter summary

This chapter looks at why it is important to classify mental disorders: it asks the question what are we trying to achieve by classifying mental disorders? As we will see, classifying disorders is very useful to help clinicians and researchers to understand the causes of these problems and to develop effective treatments. The second half of the chapter progresses to look at the classification systems that have been developed to classify mental disorders. In particular, you will be introduced to the *Diagnostic and Statistical Manual of Mental Disorders* (*DSM*). We end the chapter by thinking about whether this particular classification system is a reliable and valid system.

Assessment targets

After reading this chapter you should be able to:

Target 1: **Explain the benefits gained from classifying mental illnesses. Question 1 at the end of this chapter tests you on this.**

Target 2: **Explain the properties that a good classification should have. Question 2 at the end of this chapter tests you on this.**

Target 3: **Explain the shortcomings of systems such as DSM-IV. Question 3 at the end of this chapter tests you on this.**

Target 4: **Explain the pitfalls of trying to classify mental illness. Question 4 at the end of this chapter tests you on this.**

Section 1

Why do we classify?

The reason psychologists have spent lots of time developing complex classification systems for mental illness is because of the confusion that reigned before they were developed. Virtually every other chapter in this book will refer back, at some point, to the concepts developed in this first chapter because it's here that we'll explore the fundamental framework within which researchers and clinicians operate. This section in particular will help you to understand why classifying mental illnesses is a useful thing to do.

CRUCIAL CONCEPT
Classification is a system by which entities are divided into subclasses (or groups or categories). So it's really just grouping together entities that are the same. If we had a pile of fruit, classifying them might entail grouping together all of the apples, all of the oranges and all of the bananas – it's just the process of grouping together things that are the same.

How is classification done?

Let me talk about the things you need to think about when classifying things by using an example. Imagine you're an alien, who is trying to live a normal life on Earth. Imagine, also, that you manage to get yourself a job as a research assistant in the infant study unit at the University of Sussex. Now Dr Leavens, the head of this unit, conducts research on the pointing behaviour of infant humans and has been known to go to the zoo now and again to collect similar data on infant chimpanzees. As an alien, you've just arrived here and you don't know anything about the animals that inhabit this strange planet. To do your job properly, you need to (at the very least) be able to discriminate humans from other animals; discriminate chimpanzees from other animals; and especially discriminate humans from chimpanzees.

You might think it's pretty easy to discriminate human babies from chimpanzee babies. Let's have a look at what we'd need to know:

- **Attributes of a given entity**: an entity is just a member of a group, or subclass. What we need to know here are the attributes that humans and chimpanzees possess.

- **Defining characteristics of each subclass**: we'd also need to know a set of defining characteristics that allow us to classify entities into different groups. So we need to know what characteristics define a human and a chimp.

The problem is, how to decide on the characteristics that define a human or chimp. We could take several approaches:

- **Behavioural**: we could ask 'how do humans and chimps behave?' In adults this might be easy because humans talk and chimps don't, humans waste lots of time doing pointless things like work whereas chimps more sensibly spend their days swinging around on vines. However, in infants there aren't such obvious differences; chimps like staying close to their mother eating sweet things like fruit, don't talk and produce lots of smelly waste – the same description could equally well be applied to your average human infant!

- **Cognitive**: we could ask 'how do humans and chimps think differently?' Again, in adults this might prove fruitful: humans are capable of fairly high-level reasoning, complex language, musical and artistic creativity and can put themselves in the minds of others. However, chimps have simple language capabilities, are capable of problem-solving, and given a pot of paint and a brush are, arguably, artistically creative. Take infant humans and chimps and the distinction is even more blurred: there is limited language in both, no ability to take other perspectives and few problem-solving abilities.

- **Physical**: We could just resort to saying 'yeah, but chimps are hairier than humans, have different facial proportions (bigger ears for example) and tend not to be upright.' Admittedly, your average baby is not as hairy as a chimp, but it moves on all fours – like a chimp – and the facial proportions may be less self-evident to an alien than they are to us (bearing in mind it's important for any species to identify its own kind) because we both have two eyes, a mouth, two ears, a nose, and similar skin (compared to, say, a lizard!).

- **Biological**: The final way in which we could view the distinction is at a biological level – do we have a different genetic make up? Actually it turns out that humans and chimpanzees are 98.7% identical in their genomic DNA sequences (see Enard et al., 2002) so even these differences are small.

CRUCIAL CONCEPT

The classification process entails finding several **necessary and sufficient conditions** that allow us to accurately categorise entities into different subclasses.

In our example, you might decide that for an entity to be categorised into the subclass of 'infant chimpanzee' it is necessary that it is hairy, climbs trees and has certain genes (you'd be looking at the 1.3% of genes that differ in humans and chimps). Let's look at which are necessary conditions and which are sufficient.

Necessary conditions: these are attributes that a subclass of an object needs to have to be considered as a member of that subclass. However, this attribute alone is not sufficient to define you as a member of that subclass. So to be considered an infant chimp it might be necessary to be hairy, climb trees, like bananas, and have certain genes and we might decide that all of these attributes are necessary to be a chimp. That is, an entity has to have all four.

Sufficient conditions: these are attributes that are sufficient in their own right to make an accurate classification. So we might decide that if the necessary condition of having certain genes is met then this is sufficient to be a chimp regardless of whether this entity likes bananas or climbs trees. Conversely, we might decide that liking bananas is not a sufficient condition because lots of human babies like bananas too, so it is not a good single criterion on which to base classification.

The example I've used is supposed to illustrate the complexities inherent in trying to classify something as fundamental as the species to which an entity belongs. Imagine then how difficult it is to find the defining attributes for a complex psychological disorder. Another problem that we face is that, even assuming we can decide on the necessary and sufficient conditions for a subclass, we have to be able to measure these attributes. With something physical, measurement can be reliable and obtainable: it is, for example, possible to take gene samples although you probably don't want to resort to this every time you meet a chimp/human! However, with psychological constructs, such as mental illness, we're reliant on less objective and reliable measures. For example, can we reliably measure if a person is 'sad' and can we compare this measure in different people? These most basic issues in classification are hugely problematic, which perhaps makes you wonder why we bother classifying disorders at all.

Why classify disorders?

The short answer to the question is that we classify disorders in the hope that it allows us a basis upon which to understand and treat them. Clinical psychology is the application of scientific methods to understand and resolve human problems and classification helps us to do this. How on earth could we develop a theory of what causes schizophrenia without first deciding what schizophrenia actually is! Before classification systems existed, virtually every clinician or professor had their own ideas about classification and what constituted a given disorder (see Kendler, 1975). There are two main benefits of classification:

Classification enforces similarity within the groups we study. If a disorder is caused by the same underlying problem then we'd expect all people with this disorder to have this problem, but we wouldn't expect other people to have the problem. So if depression was caused by too little serotonin (a chemical in the brain – see Chapter 8) then we'd expect depressives to have a certain amount of serotonin and non-depressives to have more. Imagine it's an ideal world and we can simply stick people's head in a magic box and measure precisely the units of serotonin in their brain. Let's also assume that we know that the average amount of serotonin is 5 units. If we don't have a classification system, or our classification system is very bad, then we'll obtain very heterogeneous groups; that is, groups that contain a lot of variety. If our classification system is bad and we get heterogeneous groups then we probably won't be able to get at the underlying problem because our groups will contain lots of variability. To use our serotonin example, we could measure levels of serotonin and find that on average our group has 5 units of serotonin in their brains—this is no different from 'normal' levels so we could conclude that serotonin is not an important factor in depression (see Figure 1). By classifying people, we're trying to reduce this variability between people to get a group of like-minded people. If our classification system is good then we'll end up with relatively homogeneous groups. To use our serotonin example again (see Figure 1), if we measured levels in a group of like-minded people we stand more chance of detecting a difference in this group compared to the general population (so in Figure 1 we find that our homogeneous group of depressives do indeed have lower levels of serotonin). By creating homogeneous groups, it is easier to research a given disorder and to try to understand what causes it; this in turn will help us develop treatments. Without some agreement about what constitutes a particular disorder, we would be unlikely to unearth common underlying processes (because we'd be studying a heterogeneous group of people).

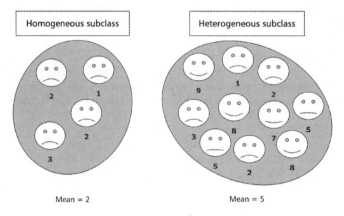

Figure 1. The importance of homogeneous subclasses

Communication between scientists: a related function of classification is that it allows scientists to communicate with other scientists, and patients and their relatives, about the theories or treatments they've developed. Without classification this wouldn't be possible because one scientist's understanding of a disorder would differ from another's.

Of course these are the advantages of classification, but as with most things there are problems too – especially when classifying mental disorders. We shall discuss some of these problems in Section 3.

How should we classify?

Without knowing it, we've already seen several things that a good classification system should have in an ideal world.

Mutually exclusive and collectively exhaustive subclasses

This just means that disorders should be distinct. Mutually exclusive means that if something belongs to one subclass it cannot belong to another: so to use our earlier example, if you're classified as a chimpanzee you shouldn't also be classified as a human—you should be one thing or the other. In mental health terms, if you're diagnosed as being depressed, then you shouldn't also be able to be diagnosed as being schizophrenic. Collectively exhaustive means that all entities can be classified into a subclass; for example, all examples of chimps on the planet Earth should be able to be classified as chimps using the criteria we've established for classification. It should not be possible to come across a chimp that cannot be classified (for example, if we just used being hairy as a single criterion for classification as a chimpanzee then we'd be stuck if we came across a bald chimp!). In mental health terms, this means that everyone who is, in reality, suffering from, say, panic disorder should be classified as having panic by our criteria. Although it might be desirable, in principle, to classify mental health problems into distinct categories, as we'll see later this isn't entirely realistic because of the complexity of psychological syndromes.

Necessary and sufficient conditions

We have already seen that there must be characteristics that are necessary for classification into a subclass. For example, to define someone as having obsessive-compulsive disorder (OCD) it may be necessary that they have intrusive thoughts. There must also be a set of sufficient conditions to belong to a subclass; for example, there may be many people without OCD who have intrusive thoughts, so this condition alone is not sufficient to have the disorder, you may need to have intrusive thoughts *and* a heightened belief that you'll act upon these thoughts.

Concept

Once the conditions of membership have been defined, the subclass must be described by some kind of concept that reflects the nature of the conditions. For example, OCD as a concept reflects the persistent and uncontrollable nature of the thoughts and actions associated with the conditions that define the disorder.

Extend the concept

Once we have a concept, it must be possible to generalise this concept and extend it to new exemplars. So if a new entity is encountered that has not previously been classified, it must be possible to classify this new exemplar based on our concept.

There has been a lot of recent debate about whether mental disorders are **discrete** or **continuous**. You can think of this distinction in terms of whether people with disorders can be neatly placed within a diagnostic 'box' or not. Does someone with a mental disorder have attributes not experienced at all by 'normal' people, or does having a mental disorder mean that some of your 'normal' attributes are experienced in some qualitatively distinct way? For example, panic disorder (see Chapter 4) is characterised by experiencing panic attacks. It's estimated that up to 40% of the population experience panic attacks at some point in their lives, so is it the case that people with panic disorder experience these attacks in a more severe way than people without panic disorder, or do they just experience them more often?

As you go through this book you'll probably experience what some people call '**medical student syndrome**', that is, as you read the diagnostic criteria for each disorder you'll probably be able to relate to at least some of the symptoms and you'll start to wonder whether you actually have that disorder! However, the chances are that you haven't, but it does show you that most of the disorders contain elements that are part of everyone's normal experience, and you'll see in the next section the various ways in which psychologists have tried to demarcate normal experience from the experiences in specific disorders.

Quick test

1. Why is it important to classify mental disorders?

2. What properties should a good classification system have?

Section 2

How are mental disorders classified?

This section looks at the actual system used for classifying mental disorders and how this system developed. Throughout this section we'll be drawing on ideas from the previous section about what constitutes a good classification system and we'll think about whether current systems for classifying mental disorders meet the requirements of a good system.

We saw in the last section that a classification system requires a set of necessary and sufficient conditions for membership to a subclass.

CRUCIAL CONCEPT

In mental illness the conditions we use are the symptoms of the disorder. A symptom can be a certain way of thinking (cognitive symptoms), a certain way of behaving (behavioural symptoms), or certain feelings (emotional or physiological symptoms). A collection of symptoms is known as a syndrome. A syndrome is just a set of symptoms that tend to occur together.

The history of modern classification systems

The idea of classifying mental illness has been around for some time; in fact, Hippocrates distinguished mania (states of excitement), melancholia (states of sadness), paranoia and epilepsy as far back as the fourth century B.C. However, the style and approach of most modern classification systems owe much to Kraepelin, who in the early 1900s was one of the first to classify distinct syndromes by making a distinction between **dementia praecox** and **manic-depressive psychosis**. Kraepelin defined these two discrete disorders using necessary and sufficient attributes for classification.

Since then two major classification systems have developed: the World Health Organisation (WHO) have developed the *International Classification of Disease* (currently in its tenth revision, ICD-10, 1992), which includes classification criteria for psychiatric problems; similarly, the American Psychiatric Association (APA) developed a set of diagnostic manuals based on the ICD system of classification, which is called the *Diagnostic and Statistical Manual of Mental Disorders* (currently in its fourth revision, *DSM–IV*, 1994). It's fair to say that *DSM* is the prevalent system in the United States, and is used frequently by psychology researchers worldwide who study clinical issues. However, there are a substantial number of clinicians who use *ICD*. In recent editions the two systems have become extremely similar and I'll focus on *DSM* throughout this book.

In 1952 the first *DSM* was published (APA, 1952); it was based largely on the clinical observations and interpretation of the research literature of a small committee of leading clinicians and researchers. Some years later proposed revisions to *DSM-I* were reviewed by a different committee resulting in *DSM-II* (APA, 1968). These early examples differ substantially from the current version in that they were much more driven by psychodynamic thinking (see Chapter 2) and offered not only descriptive features of disorders, but suggestions of the cause of the disorder. Possibly the biggest overhaul of *DSM* came in the mid-1970s when a committee was appointed to revise the manual to take account of research innovations. Their remit was to rely as much as possible on research evidence to increase the diagnostic validity of the manual (see Spitzer, Williams & Skodol, 1980). However, given the relative lack of research evidence it was not always possible to resolve differences of opinion by using objective data (see Widiger & Clark, 2000).

The end result was a *DSM* in which there were criteria that were not always clear or consistent and were, at times, contradictory (as acknowledged by the APA in their revision of *DSM–III*). The revised version, *DSM-III-R* (APA, 1987) made more effort to systematically draw upon the research literature and field trials were conducted to test proposed criteria for certain disorders. Shortly after this revision surfaced, a committee was already in place to work on the next edition. *DSM-IV* is much more based on the *ICD* ideals about how data should be assimilated into diagnostic criteria, and this is why the two manuals have become more similar over time. Suggested changes to be included in *DSM-IV* were considered using extensive literature reviews, and including studies that had sufficient methodological information to allow confidence in the results (see Widiger & Clark, 2000 for a review).

CRUCIAL CONCEPT

DSM–IV is based on a **multiaxial system** and contains five axes. The first two axes primarily deal with diagnostic considerations.

Axis I contains all diagnostic categories except personality disorders and mental retardation, which appear on **Axis II**. As such, the clinician uses Axes I and II to make a diagnosis based on symptom information.

The remaining three axes are primarily to allow clinicians to collect social and medical information and to code this information in an appropriate way.

Axis III is for collecting information about general medical conditions and physical health, and **Axis IV** is for gathering information about psychosocial and environmental problems (such as family or work-related problems).

The final axis, **Axis V**, is a general measure of adaptive functioning (GAFS) that can range from 1 (suicidal behaviour, persistent violence etc.) to 100 (symptom-free and functioning perfectly across a range of activities), with stages in between including 20 (some danger of hurting oneself or others or gross communication impairment), 50 (serious symptoms and difficulty in functioning) and 70 (some mild symptoms or difficulty in functioning).

All the disorders we cover in this book are found on Axis I, which contains the following disorders:

- **Disorders usually first diagnosed in infancy, childhood or adolescence**: these include childhood behavioural problems, and problems with social and cognitive development. However, mental retardation is included in Axis II.

- **Delirium, dementia, amnesia and other cognitive disorders**: these are disorders caused by brain damage or deterioration.

- **Substance related disorders**: these are disorders in which the abuse of drugs has led to psychological distress.

- **Schizophrenia and other psychotic disorders**: these disorders are characterised by a detachment from reality and severe emotional and social disturbances (see Chapter 9).

- **Mood disorders**: these include depression, which is characterised by low self-esteem and extreme unhappiness, and bi-polar disorders in which these depressive episodes are broken up by periods of mania, which entail excessive engagement in enjoyable but detrimental behaviours (see Chapter 8).

- **Anxiety disorders**: these include extreme fear of specific objects or situations (specific phobias – Chapter 3), persistent and disturbing panic attacks (panic disorder – Chapter 4), fear of social situations (social phobia – Chapter 4), excessive worry (generalised anxiety disorder – Chapter 5), and persistent obsessional thoughts accompanied by ritualistic behaviour (obsessive compulsive disorder – Chapter 6).

- **Somatoform disorders**: this is a disorder in which psychological distress causes preoccupation with bodily sensations or physical symptoms. This can be either experiencing medical complaints, such as limb paralysis, without any medical explanation (**conversion disorders**) or seeking treatment for medical complaints that don't exist (**somatisation disorders**).

- **Dissociative disorders**: these are disorders such as dissociative identity disorder in which the person's usual identity is replaced by one or more alternative identities.

- **Sexual and gender identity disorders**: these include disorders of sexual performance such as premature ejaculation, male erectile dysfunction, anorgasmia and vaginismus (see Field, in press), and disorders in which sexual pleasure is gained through bizarre or illegal activities (known as **paraphilias**). Paraphilias includes necrophilia, paedophilia, voyeurism and exhibitionism.

- **Eating disorders**: these include anorexia nervosa and bulimia nervosa (see Chapter 7).

- **Sleeping disorders**: these can include disorders that interfere with sleep (insomnia) as well as sleepwalking and night terrors.

- **Impulse control disorders not elsewhere classified**: these include pyromania and obsessive gambling.
- **Adjustment disorders**: this is a failure to deal with stressful events.

Axis II contains personality disorders (disorders involving maladaptive personality traits) and mental retardation (an intellectual deficit that is present during infancy and remains throughout life). Personality disorders include antisocial personality disorders, which are characterised by a disregard for others' rights and feelings and include psychopathic disorders, dependent personality disorder, which is characterised by fear of abandonment and indecisiveness, and borderline personality disorder, which is characterised by out-of-control emotions that cannot be smoothed, hypersensitivity to abandonment, self-harm and emptiness.

Diagnoses are made on the basis of all five axes. So a person can be diagnosed with depression (Axis I), with mental retardation (Axis II), with no medical problems (Axis III), but unable to work (Axis IV), and serious symptoms and difficulty in functioning (50 on Axis V).

Quick test

1. What is *DSM*?
2. How has *DSM* changed over the years?
3. How are the five Axes of *DSM* used?

Section 3

Assessing *DSM-IV*

A good classification system needs to be both reliable and valid. Reliability refers to the fact that if different clinicians diagnosed the same person, that person should always be classified in the same way. A system is not reliable if one clinician classifies someone as having obsessive-compulsive disorder whereas another classifies the same person as schizophrenic. Reliability is necessary for validity, but it is not sufficient. In general terms, the use of standardised interview techniques and more explicit criteria in *DSM* has improved its reliability. The validity of a classification can come from many sources. At a simple level we could ask whether the diagnostic criteria have intuitive validity: do they describe the disorders in an intuitively accurate way? Other issues are whether we can isolate causal factors for a given disorder (**etiological validity**): can we predict future outcomes based on what we know about the disorder (**predictive validity**), and does the diagnosis correlate with other measures (e.g. does the classification of depression correlate with scores on questionnaires that purport to measure depression, such as Beck's Depression Inventory, *BDI*)? So is *DSM* reliable and valid?

Criticisms of *DSM*

Historically, *DSM* has been a very unreliable measure with *DSM-I* leading to only 54% agreement between therapists in diagnosis (Beck, Ward, Mandelson, Moch & Erlbaugh, 1962) and recent manuals (*DSM-III* and *DSM-III-R*) improving this value to only 70% (Kirk & Kutchins, 1992). Over the years many criticisms have been levelled at *DSM*.

Specificity

We saw earlier that one idea of a classification system is to produce mutually exclusive groups of people, yet there is considerable co-occurrence between disorders. (You'll sometimes see co-occurrence between disorders referred to as **comorbidity**, however there has been a shift away from this term in recent years.) For example, if you look at panic disorder patients around 33% will report a prior episode of depression and 35% report concurrent generalised anxiety disorder (Ball, Otto, Pollack & Rosenbaum, 1994). Other studies have shown that the lifetime co-occurrence between depression and anxiety can be as high as 73.1% (Lewinsohn, Zinbarg, Seeley, Lewinsohn & Sack, 1997). Also, if you look at the symptoms of disorders like **borderline personality disorder** (see above) you'll notice that they are also benchmarks of depression. There is also some evidence from an extensive longitudinal study that the frequent co-occurrence of disorders doesn't represent symptom overlap but that there are core pathological processes (Krueger, Caspi, Moffitt & Silva, 1998). This just means that it could be that there are core processes, for example a tendency to dwell on negative aspects of life; the effect that this process has is influenced by other genetic traits, possibly other pathological processes and environmental stressors (see Widiger & Clark, 2000).

Cultural and gender biases

Szasz (1971) argued that abnormality does not really exist and that *DSM* reflects a societal desire to suppress individuals whose behaviour does not conform to our socially constructed norms. This is highlighted by culture-bound syndromes, which are syndromes specific to certain cultures (see Simons and Hughes, 1985 for a review). For example *koro*, or genital retraction syndrome (GRS) is a culture-bound syndrome that occurs in Malaysia, Indonesia and China. Sufferers of *koro* believe that their genitals (or in the case of women, breasts and/or genitals) are retracting into the body and local tradition upholds the belief that the end result is death. This delusion is rooted in cultural metaphysics: the *yin/yang* equilibrium, which is believed to exist when a husband has sex with his wife, is perceived to be disturbed by unhealthy or abnormal sexual acts (such as masturbation, nocturnal emissions, or sex with someone other than one's wife or husband). This loss of *yang* manifests itself in penis or genital shrinkage. There have even been epidemics of *koro* such as in Singapore in 1967. Similarly, *DSM* has been criticised for adopting a male-dominated perspective on disorders. For example, *dependent personality disorder*, which is characterised by fear of abandonment and indecisiveness is said to pathologise normal female behaviour because it doesn't conform to male perceptions of normality.

Stigma

Rosenhan (1973) elegantly demonstrated that diagnostic labels change perceptions of the person. Over some time he got eight 'normal' people to report to 12 psychiatric hospitals with symptoms of hearing voices saying 'empty', 'hollow' and 'thud'. All were diagnosed as schizophrenic. However, Rosenhan reported that subsequent to their diagnosis, doctors and staff treated these pseudopatients differently; for example, staff would ignore the pseudopatients' attempts at conversation, their normal histories were distorted into tales of ambivalent relationships and outbursts were attributed to the pathology and not the behaviour of staff, and so on.

Political influence

Some of the disorders included (and excluded) in *DSM* are the result of political agendas. For example, **post-traumatic stress disorder** was included after Vietnam soldiers protested for its inclusion so that they could receive sickness benefit. Similarly, **homosexuality** was considered a mental disorder in *DSM-I* and *DSM-II*. It was dropped partly because of the controversy of its inclusion and the ensuing pressure from gay rights groups. Although there are few of our generation (I hope) who would consider homosexuality a mental disorder, only relatively recently it would have been considered just that (let's not forget it was a criminal act less than a century ago!). This demonstrates how cultural and historical perceptions of 'abnormality' influence what we consider to be mental illness, and this in turn influences the diagnostic tools that we develop. Another example was **masochistic personality disorder**, which was going to be included as a disorder characterised by a person persistently getting into and remaining in situations in which others use and abuse them. However, some psychologists felt that it would serve to pathologise women in abusive relationships (Caplan & Gans, 1991). One solution was to propose a second disorder, **sadistic personality disorder**, which was characterised by a need to abuse others (and hence would pathologise the abuser). However, this too is problematic because it allows abusers legal protection through diminished responsibility. Both disorders were appended to *DSM-III-R* as disorders needing further study but were both dropped in *DSM-IV*.

Homogeneity of sufferers

Classification imposes homogeneity within disorders and encourages therapists to ignore the individual characteristics of a particular patient. This can be problematic because not everyone is the same, and not everyone will respond well to a fixed therapeutic regime. In this respect classification may be more useful to researchers, for whom homogeneity is desirable, than to clinicians who need to bear in mind the individual components of a given person's problem.

To sum up, *DSM* has come under fire from many people for the way it's been constructed. Undoubtedly the system has improved since it was first introduced, and the introduction of more rigorous attention to research findings has produced a useful, but not perfect, tool for clinicians and researchers.

Quick test

1. Is *DSM* a reliable and valid system of classification?

2. What are some of the biases in *DSM*?

Section 4

End of chapter assessment

Questions

1. Why do we classify mental disorders?

2. What should we strive for in a good classification system?

3. Is *DSM* a reliable and valid system of classification?

4. Can we ever achieve an adequate system for classifying mental disorders?

Section 5

Further reading

American Psychiatric Association (1994). *Diagnostic and Statistical Manual of Mental Disorders* (4th ed.). Washington, DC: Author. (The best way to get a feel for how *DSM* actually works is to have a look at a copy!).

Widiger, T. A., & Clark, L. A. (2000). Towards *DSM-V* and the classification of psychopathology. *Psychological Bulletin, 126*, 946–963. (This is a wonderful overview of the development of *DSM* and where it might go in the future.)

Chapter 2
Approaches to mental illness

Chapter summary

We saw in the last chapter that classifying mental disorders is a an extremely difficult thing to do; explaining them is even harder. This chapter overviews four of the dominant approaches to clinical psychology: **psychodynamic**, **behavioural**, **cognitive** and **biological**. First, we overview the basic ideas behind **psychoanalysis** and **Freudian theory**, before looking at how the shortcomings of these ideas led to a focus on behavioural aspects of mental illness. In this approach, mental illness is seen merely as the product of maladaptive learning, and although this proved an extremely fruitful idea, its shortcomings soon became apparent and led clinicians and researchers to look at how people with mental disorders actually think – not just how they behave. Finally, we overview some key concepts behind biological explanations of mental illness.

Assessment targets

After reading this chapter you should be able to:

Target 1: Explain psychodynamic approaches to mental illness and the basics of treatment. Question 1 at the end of this chapter tests you on this.

Target 2: Explain behavioural models of mental illness and the treatments deriving from them. Question 2 at the end of this chapter tests you on this.

Target 3: Explain the cognitive approach to mental illness and how this model translates into therapy. Question 3 at the end of this chapter tests you on this.

Target 4: Describe the ways in which behavioural and cognitive approaches to mental illness are complementary. Question 4 at the end of this chapter tests you on this.

Target 5: Explain the basic biological concepts such as neurotransmission and brain systems such as the limbic system. Question 5 at the end of this chapter tests you on this.

Target 6: Explain biological approaches to mental illness. Question 6 at the end of this chapter tests you on this.

Section 1

Psychodynamic approaches

This section will explore psychodynamic approaches to mental illness by first looking at Freud's theories, and then his treatment ideas. Finally, we'll look at whether this approach still has value in psychology and exactly what contribution Freud made to modern clinical psychology.

Freud's theory

Summing up the wealth of Freud's ideas is no easy task, but essentially his whole theoretical framework revolved around the simple idea that everyone has conflicts between **unconscious desires and drives**, and **conscious behaviours and actions**. This idea is perhaps Freud's biggest contribution to modern psychology. Freud's early conceptions of neurotic behaviour were that it stemmed from some kind of traumatic early experience that the patient had buried deep in their unconscious. Freud worked with Breuer (1842–1925) between around 1888 and 1893–6 using **hypnosis** as a way of unlocking the unconscious to allow the patient to exorcise this buried trauma by expressing appropriate emotional responses to it (hypnosis was used as a cathartic process). Freud developed these techniques but eventually dropped hypnosis in favour of **free association**, which ultimately led to a split between him and Breuer.

CRUCIAL CONCEPTS

Free association: a technique whereby a patient is taught to talk freely without censoring any thoughts. Rather like just saying anything that comes into your head. It's thought to reveal preoccupations of which the patient is unaware.

Oedipal complex: named after Sophocles' drama about King Oedipus who unwittingly kills his own father and marries his own mother. In Freudian terms it reflects everyone's destiny to 'direct our first sexual impulse towards our mother and our first hatred and our first murderous wish towards our father' (Freud, 1954, p. 262).

Electra complex: this is related to the Oedipus complex but happens in girls and centres on them having their father as a love interest and conflict with their mother.

The death of Freud's father in 1896, and his ambivalence to it, undoubtedly had a profound effect on his thinking. He went into a period of self-analysis, which in part he used to try to unearth the mystery of why the unconscious mind often seemed reluctant to become conscious. His answer was that the unconscious was primarily concerned with primitive desires and wishes such as eating, drinking, having sex and pleasure of any description. A person's primitive desires were later given the name of the **id** by Freud. During Freud's self-analysis he came up with several revelations regarding child sexuality. He claimed that children went through a series of developmental stages during which they were fixated with various pleasurable activities:

- 0–1 was the **oral stage** during which activity centres on pleasures derived from the mouth (hence why babies will put anything and everything in their mouths);
- following this the **anal stage** develops (1–2 years old) during which the child discovers that toilet activities are really quite enjoyable;
- the **phallic stage** (3–6) then materialises during which the child discovers that they have genitals and that they can be a lot of fun too.

Freud believed that most children would enter and subsequently resolve these stages. However, failure to resolve a stage would lead the person to become trapped within it, which would lead to subsequent neurosis. For example, failure to resolve the oral stage would lead to oral fixation (such as smoking, excessive drinking, or eating disorders), and failure to resolve the anal stage would lead to excessive control and hoarding (obsessive compulsive disorder). The most interesting stage is perhaps the phallic stage, in which Freud postulated that young boys developed an Oedipal complex, in which they become attracted to their mothers and see their fathers as sexual competitors. They become jealous of their fathers and start to worry that their fathers, realising the sexual threat from their son, might castrate them. Most boys resolve this conflict by identifying with their father's attitudes and behaviours but Freud argued that if this hostility towards the father remained unresolved it transferred to a more socially appropriate target (for example, an animal). The female equivalent was the Electra complex, in which girls, like boys, first identify their mother as a love interest but soon realise that they cannot fulfil this love without a penis. Freud argued that girls develop penis envy, which focuses their attention on their fathers. The father becomes something of a love interest (arguably because the girl is trying to gain control of a penis, or perhaps desires a baby as a penis substitute – Freud played around with various ideas but never reached a satisfactory conclusion), and the mother becomes the object of jealousy. Ultimately Freud didn't work out the Electra complex very well at all, because he wanted the girl to end up identifying with her mother, and to have some anxiety along the way but, unlike in the Oedipus complex, the mother couldn't cut off a penis that doesn't exist so there's no potential for unresolved anxiety. Also, if the penis envy just goes away of its own accord then it raises the question of what function it served in the first place!

Needless to say there are numerous problems with these theories, not least of which that it is very gender-biased: why should girls feel that they are lacking a penis rather than boys wondering why they have this curious additional bit of anatomy!

The final stage in Freud's thinking was to develop his earlier ideas of the id. He proposed two other systems in the mind: the **super-ego**, which is a person's morality or conscience, and the **ego**, which is a reality-checking device. These systems were seen to be in perpetual conflict with the id wishing to do things, the super-ego telling it that it can't, and the ego stuck in between trying to compromise between the two.

Psychoanalysis

Therapeutically, Freud initially used hypnosis (regression to a childhood state) as a means to unlock early traumatic experiences. As I've suggested though, he moved away to other techniques such as **dream analysis** and the '**talking cure**' (free association) to unearth the cause of trauma. Dream analysis was based on the idea that unconscious desires would manifest themselves in dreams. Therapy involved patients recalling their dreams and Freud offering detailed analysis of these dreams in terms of psychodynamic ideas. These interpretations centred on **symbolism**, that is, characters and situations in the dreams were seen as representing other things. For example, a woman dreamt that her child was sent away by her mother before the pair of them boarded a train that subsequently ran the child over. The woman reproached her mother for having sent her child off alone. This was interpreted as the child representing the woman's genitals and the reproachment of her mother represented her resentment at being 'expected to live as though she had no genitals' (Freud, 1954, p. 363). In other words, she was annoyed at her mother for wanting her to live a sexless life. A literal translation might alternatively be that the woman was just anxious about her daughter being harmed.

Therapies involving these kinds of techniques can last up to eight years, and quite obviously involve huge amounts of subjective interpretation and guidance on the part of the therapist. The guiding principle though is that some deep-seated issues need to be unlocked by the therapist for the patient to be able to resolve these issues and move on.

Evidence for psychodynamic theories

The major problem with Freud's ideas is that they are unfalsifiable because the theory offers no predictions about behaviour. It was based on single case studies and so has no scientific basis and stems largely from Freud's own self-analysis. Presumably, had Freud had less issues of his own regarding his father, his theory would have looked very different. In terms of therapy, many have attempted to show the benefit of psychodynamic approaches. Smith, Glass and Miller (1980) famously summarised the wealth of studies that had been conducted and concluded that psychotherapy was consistently beneficial in numerous ways. However, as Eysenck (1985) points out, these claims are not substantiated by the data Smith *et al.* present and this observation reiterated his earlier conclusions

(Eysenck, 1952) that neurotic people tend to get better if you leave them alone anyway. (In fact, he claimed, two thirds of neurotics would consider themselves cured two years later without any intervention – a sentiment that Rachman and Wilson endorsed in another major review of psychotherapy in 1980.) Supporters of psychotherapy typically quote studies that do show benefits from psychotherapy, but as Eysenck (1985) elegantly demonstrates these studies often have major flaws such as not utilising control groups who do not undergo therapy, or failing to include those who drop out of therapy on the rather dubious assumption that they would have got better had they continued in therapy!

What does Freud have to offer?

We've really only scratched the surface of Freud's ideas, but I hope to have demonstrated that these ideas are difficult to test and arguably have led to therapies with little demonstrated clinical efficacy. Does this mean Freud has nothing to offer? Well, no, in a sense he did an amazing amount for psychology in identifying the unconscious and starting scientists thinking about alternative models (I suspect his lack of scientific rigour and experimentation also did much to expedite experimental psychology as critics rushed to produce scientifically testable alternative theories!). However, Freud's often intuitively understood theories have also left psychology with scars to bear in that most people's perceptions of therapy are probably based on psychoanalysis, which although still widely practised, is probably not the treatment of choice for many disorders. Having said this, there are people who still find psychodynamic therapies hugely beneficial (I usually get told this after lectures in which I've just spent an hour criticising Freud), but the cynic in me still wonders whether they would have resolved their own issues anyway, or whether they simply need someone (trained or untrained) to listen.

Quick test

1. How did Freud explain mental illness?

2. What are Freud's psychosexual stages?

3. What are the id, ego and superego?

4. What techniques are used in psychodynamic therapy and is there any evidence that they work?

Section 2

Behavioural models

Behavioural models of mental illness grew out of an increasing frustration with Freud's unscientific ideas. John Watson was a hugely influential psychologist whose work in the early 1900s, along with Ivan Pavlov's work on reflexive learning, did much to inspire the likes of Wolpe and Eysenck who laid the foundations (and built most of the building for that matter) for **behaviour therapy** (see Rachman, 1997 for a historical review). This section explores the theory behind behavioural models and how these translate into therapy.

The behaviourist perspective on mental illness

The basic idea behind behavioural models is that mental illness is learned; that is, abnormal behaviour results from learning abnormal responses to the environment. The mechanism behind this learning is **classical conditioning** (also known as **associative learning** – see Davey and Field, in press, for an introduction).

CRUCIAL CONCEPTS

A **conditioned stimulus**, or **CS**, is a stimulus that initially evokes no response, but comes to evoke a response through conditioning. It can be thought of as a predictor.

An **unconditioned stimulus**, or **UCS**, is a biologically significant stimulus that initially evokes a reflexive response such as salivation, fear, happiness.

An **unconditioned response**, or **UCR**, is the reflexive response elicited by an unconditioned stimulus, such as salivation or a change in heart rate.

A **conditioned response**, or **CR**, is a response elicited by a conditioned stimulus after conditioning. So, it is a learnt response.

Conditioning is the process through which a conditioned stimulus comes to evoke a response through being associated with an unconditioned stimulus. In pragmatic terms, the CS is presented followed shortly after by the UCS, so the organism learns that the CS predicts the UCS.

Conditioning was first discovered in the early 1900s by the Russian physiologist Pavlov, but only really came to the attention of the Western world in 1927 when his work became available in English. In a prototypical conditioning experiment there are initially two stimuli.

- The first stimulus (in Pavlov's case a bell) ordinarily evokes no response and is called the **conditioned stimulus**, or **CS**. It is called the conditioned stimulus because it initially evokes no response and so any response it comes to evoke is due to conditioning. The CS can be thought of as a predictor.

- The second stimulus is called the **unconditioned stimulus (UCS)**, and is so called because it naturally evokes an unlearned, reflexive response known as an **unconditioned response (UCR)**. The UCS can be thought of as an outcome or consequence.

In Pavlov's experiment the UCS, or outcome, was some powdered dog food that elicited a salivation reflex (the UCR). During an experiment the dog hears the bell and shortly afterwards receives the food, which causes it to salivate. In technical terminology we say that the CS is paired in close temporal contiguity with the UCS on several occasions. After several pairings the dog starts to salivate merely at the sound of the bell. Previously the bell elicited no response, therefore this new response has been learnt by the dog and is so-called the **conditioned response**, or **CR**.

In terms of mental illness, the idea is simply that a person learns mental illness through associating some stimulus with some other stimulus, which is unpleasant. For example, a woman who was scared of buttons remembered picking up a metal button that was next to a fire and had become very hot. The fear was learnt through associating buttons with the pain she felt when she picked up that metal button. I'll expand on these ideas in more detail in Chapter 3 (specific phobias). Behavioural models are, in a sense, the antithesis of psychoanalysis in that the subjective and intrapersonal explanations are gone in favour of simple reflexive learning. Responses are not cognitively mediated; they are not due to unconscious desires, drives, or unresolved conflicts, but simply that you've learnt an inappropriate response to a stimulus.

Behaviour therapy
We've seen that the behavioural model basically suggests that mental illness results from maladaptive learning processes. As such, the model simply assumes that by treating the learnt behaviour, you treat the underlying cause. As such, therapy hinges on relearning. There are three crucial concepts here.

—— CRUCIAL CONCEPTS ——

Exposure is the treatment of anxiety through a person interacting with the thing they fear (either in their imagination or in real life).

A **graded hierarchy** is an ordered list of feared situations that range from a situation that evokes very little fear to a situation that evokes intense anxiety or discomfort.

Systematic desensitisation is a therapeutic technique whereby a patient is taught to relax and is then asked to imagine the situations in their graded hierarchy (starting at the least fearful) while in this state of relaxation.

Wolpe (1958, 1961, 1962) pioneered various techniques for eliminating anxious responses through relearning. We'll look in considerably more detail at the practicalities of this form of therapy in the next chapter (as it is particularly useful in treating specific phobias), so in this section I'll restrict myself to some general principles. All therapy is based on **exposure** of some sort. Exposing someone to the thing they fear has a simple, yet powerful, effect: it enhances their anxiety at first but after reaching a peak anxiety falls. So even merely forcing someone to face something they fear for an appropriately long amount of time would make them calm (eventually) and therefore they would learn to associate that stimulus with feelings of calm rather than anxiety. In its most primitive form, **flooding**, this is exactly what happens: a phobic is exposed to the stimulus of which they are scared and are prevented from escape or avoidance of the stimulus. Over time, their fear response diminishes.

However, more sophisticated methods have been developed than flooding, which rely on **counter-conditioning** (that is replacing one response with another). One way is to use a **graded hierarchy** in which the patient (e.g. a mouse phobic) thinks of several situations from a minimal fear situation (i.e. a mouse running around in a big field) to a maximum fear intensity situation (i.e. mouse running up their trouser leg). In **systematic desensitisation** (Wolpe, 1961) the patient is taught how to relax and is asked to practise the relaxation techniques at home until they can reach a certain degree of relaxation. In the therapy itself, the patient is asked to relax and a neutral scene is imagined before moving on to the lowest situation in the graded hierarchy generated earlier (this can be done using the imagination, or using real situations). Subsequent sessions begin with the patient imagining the highest situation in the hierarchy that could be imagined without fear at the previous session before moving on to the next situation in the hierarchy. The sessions are ended when the highest situation in the graded hierarchy can be imagined, or confronted in reality, without anxiety (see Chapter 3 for more detail).

Quick test

1. What is Pavlovian conditioning?

2. How can Pavlovian learning explain mental illnesses?

3. How can we use Pavlovian conditioning to help people with mental illnesses to un-learn their maladaptive behaviour?

Section 3

Cognitive models

In the 1970s there was something of a backlash against behavioural explanations of mental illness. This was partly because the shortfalls of the behavioural explanations became clearer (see Chapter 3), but also because clinicians such as Aaron Beck were making it increasingly clear that people with psychiatric problems have different thoughts to people who don't have these problems. Pure behaviourists believed that thoughts were unimportant, and so the growing evidence that people with psychiatric problems did think differently undermined the notion that these problems could be explained in purely behavioural terms. This section looks at what a **cognitive bias** is, and the types of cognitive biases found in psychiatric disorders.

─── CRUCIAL CONCEPT ───

A **cognitive bias** is a distortion in the way that someone thinks about or perceives a situation.

Types of cognitive bias

Cognitive theories are based on the idea that psychiatric problems are caused by cognitive biases or maladaptive thinking. In behavioural models thoughts are ignored; therefore, to treat a disorder phobia you simply treat the learnt behaviour. Cognitive theories are really the opposite in that they assume that cognitive biases drive the phobia and cause the fear response. Therefore, if you treat the cognitions, the behaviour will vanish.

Most research into cognitive biases looks at the way in which information is processed (**information-processing biases**) and these can include biases in attention, memory, thinking and judgments.

Attention

An attentional bias can be either an urge to fixate your attention on a certain kind of stimulus, or it can be a need to disengage attention from certain kinds of stimuli. A good example of an attentional bias is a task called the **emotional stroop** task. In this task, participants are presented with several words that are written in different colours. The task is to name the colour of the word. Experimenters can manipulate the types of words used to see whether they distract certain people more than others. For example, you could use emotionally neutral words (e.g. plate) and spider-related words (e.g. fangs, hairy). If someone takes longer to name the colour of one type of word it means that they are too busy focusing on what the word means to name its colour – the word itself distracts them from the colour-naming task. So we might expect that spider phobic people are more distracted by the spider words than non-arachnophobic people and so take longer to name their colours (Kindt & Brosschot, 1997). This would show an attentional bias towards spider words.

Memory recall

A given cue can trigger any one of many memories. People with depression are more likely to recall negative memories to a given cue than people who don't have depression. This is because depressed mood (in depressed people, or in non-depressed people into whom a negative mood is induced) slows down the retrieval of positive memories (see Williams, 2001). In addition, Williams has noted that depressed people consistently recall very general memories. For example, a cue of 'sorry' might elicit a fairly specific memory from a non-depressed person (e.g. 'when I upset my mother last Wednesday by forgetting to send her a birthday card') but will elicit only a general memory from a depressed person (e.g. 'when I do things wrong').

Misinterpretation

Most of us have probably misinterpreted information at some point in our lives. For example, if I walked into a room and heard someone say 'Oh, Andy is going to be dead ... .' I could interpret that as being the end of the sentence and that the person is going to kill me. However, it's possible that they were going to say 'Oh, Andy is going to be dead pleased with this Weezer CD that I've bought him' before I interrupted them. These sorts of biases happen all the time (how many times have you thought that people were talking about or laughing at you when in reality they probably weren't?). People with anxiety (Chapter 5) and depression (Chapter 8) typically make negative interpretations more than people without these disorders.

25

Perseveration

Repeatedly thinking (or churning over) thoughts in your mind is known as rumination. Many psychological problems are characterised by this kind of perseverative and iterative thought process. For example, social phobics (see Chapter 4) tend to dwell negatively upon social situations after they occur, anxious people tend to worry (which itself is a perseverative and iterative thought process – see Chapter 5) more than non-anxious people, and depressives also tend to ruminate more than non-depressed people (Watkins & Baracaia, 2001).

Quick test

1. What is the cognitive approach to mental disorders?
2. What is a cognitive bias and what forms can it take?

Section 4

Biogical models

Most of Western medicine is based on the idea that illness has an organic cause: if we have a runny nose and a cough it is because our body is retaliating against a virus, and if our leg hurts it could be because we have torn a muscle. Likewise, psychological problems could stem from physical problems. Given that what we perceive, what we feel and literally what we are stems from our brain, biological models obviously centre on problems in the brain. This section looks at a few basic biological processes and the ways in which they might go wrong.

A quick guide to the brain

Neurons and how they communicate

The average human brain contains around 100 billion **neurons**. These neurons are the building blocks of the nervous system and although you don't really have to know too much about what they are, what they look like or how they work, it is very important that you know that they talk to each other. Of course, they don't talk to each other like you and I do. However, they do pass signals to one another using their own special language. This language is known as a **neurotransmitter**, and just as there are several languages that humans use, there are several neurotransmitters in the brain. So, just like we may speak English, French or German, neurons can speak using different neurotransmitters. Some examples of neurotransmitters are dopamine, serotonin and gamma-aminobutyric acid (GABA). These neurotransmitters are just chemical substances that allow a message to pass from one neuron to another (a bit like how a language helps us humans to pass messages to each other). The actual message is in the form of an a **nerve impulse**.

Why do neurons need to use neurotransmitters? There are tiny gaps between neurons called **synaptic gaps** (or **synapses** for short). A nerve impulse can't pass through this gap so if a neuron wants to communicate with another neuron it has to fill this gap with neurotransmitter. It squirts some neurotransmitter into the gap allowing the message (the nerve impulse) to pass to the next neuron. Once the message has been sent, the synapse has to be emptied. There are two crucial processes involved in this: **reuptake** and **degradation**.

CRUCIAL CONCEPTS

A **nerve Impulse** is a change in the electrical potential of a neuron.

Reuptake is where the neurotransmitter in the synapse is reabsorbed into the neuron that sent the message.

Degradation is where the neuron receiving the message releases an enzyme that breaks down the neurotransmitter in the synapse.

Brain systems

If neurons are the building blocks of the brain, then it must surely have some 'buildings'. In fact, there are many structures that have been identified in the brain. It's easiest to think of the brain in terms of three layers:

- a **central core**
- the **limbic system**
- and the **cerebrum**.

The central core is really where the spinal cord meets the brain. This whole system can, broadly speaking, be thought of as dealing with basic primitive functioning. For example, it contains the **cerebellum**, which deals primarily with movement, but has also been implicated in reflexive learning such as conditioning (see Legg, 1989). Two other key structures in this core are the **thalamus** and **hypothalamus**. The thalamus is like a relay station and especially relays messages from sense receptors (e.g. vision, hearing, taste and touch) to the cerebrum, where they are processed. The hypothalamus is a smaller structure but no less important. In fact, this structure is thought to control basic functions such as eating, drinking and sexual activity. Stimulating different parts of the hypothalamus also causes sensations of pain and pleasure.

The limbic system sits snugly around the central core, and in particular is closely connected to the hypothalamus. This area is relatively large in mammals compared to animals such as fish and reptiles and so it's thought to regulate the primitive functions of the hypothalamus. So, for example, while you'll rarely see fish or reptiles being distracted from important duties such as eating, killing, running away or procreating, mammals appear to inhibit these urges when required. One important structure in the limbic system is the **hippocampus**, which is very important in forming memories. The limbic system also seems to have a crucial role in emotion: for example, damage to this area can lead to increased aggression. Importantly, neurons in the limbic system use noradrenergic neurotransmitters for communication: these neurotransmitters are **norepinephrine**, **serotonin**, and **dopamine**. You'll find that these neurotransmitters crop up time and time again throughout this book because they are implicated in many psychological disorders.

The final layer of the brain is the cerebrum (which includes the cerebral cortex). This part of the brain is very highly developed in humans and, without going into lots of detail about its structure, this seems to be the 'interpretation centre' of the brain. It is in these areas that we have visual areas (for interpreting what we see) and auditory areas (where we interpret what we hear) and motor areas (where we interpret what we feel) – you get the gist! You shouldn't think that these areas are independent. In fact, although some structures are quite discrete, many of them blur into the areas around them and it's often hard to tell where one structure starts and the other ends. Also, the different areas are connected to one another in all manner of complex ways.

A final thing about the brain is that it is full of holes. I know, you're probably all worried at the thought of your brain being like Swiss cheese, but it is. These holes are called **ventricles**, and they are filled with fluid.

What can go wrong in the brain?

The biological model basically suggests that psychological problems are caused by problems in the brain. So what could possibly go wrong with one of the most complex structures in the universe?

Structural abnormalities: if the ventricles in the brain are particularly large this implies that these 'holes' are taking up space that would otherwise be occupied with brain tissue. So psychopathology could be attributed to unusually sized ventricles.

Hormones: disorders could be due to abnormal levels of certain hormones (for example the secretion of cortisol during stress). The hypothalamus has a central role in controlling hormone secretion, so if this structure goes haywire then you could end up with too many or too few hormones rushing around your body.

Neurology: if the processes of degradation and reuptake go wrong you end up with either too much or too little neurotransmitter in your synapses. These chemicals might be causes of the symptoms of psychological problems.

Genetics: any of the above problems could result from genetic factors (inherited structural abnormalities, hormone imbalances or neurological factors). We can look at genetic factors to see whether they predict psychological problems.

Biological therapy

The answer to any of these problems is to sort out the organic problem. Some techniques that have traditionally been used are **psychosurgery** (surgery on the part of the brain thought to be at the root of the problem) or **electro-convulsive therapy** (**ECT**). ECT is where a seizure is induced by passing 70–130 volts of electricity through a patient's brain (this used to be done to both sides of the brain but nowadays is typically administered only to the nondominant right hemisphere). ECT is typically used only on severely depressed individuals, and psychosurgery would also be a last resort to a problem. By far the most common solution is to administer drugs aimed at increasing or reducing levels of neurotransmitters in the brain. This can be done in numerous ways: increase the production of a neurotransmitter, prevent reuptake or degradation of a neurotransmitter, and encourage reuptake or degradation of a neurotransmitter. Drugs can also be used to redress hormonal imbalances. The important thing when evaluating drugs is to compare the effect of the drug while controlling for psychological factors; this is done using what's called a placebo treatment.

CRUCIAL CONCEPT

A **placebo treatment** is a treatment designed to make the patient believe they are being treated when, in fact, the intervention has no therapeutic value. An example of a placebo would be if you gave someone a white pill made of sugar to cure their headache and told them it was an aspirin; sugar has no beneficial effect on headaches, but the patient would believe they were being treated because they think the pill is aspirin.

In any clinical trial testing the effect of a drug it is important to have a group of people who think they are taking the drug, but are in fact taking something that has no effect. All patients must believe they are taking the drug and, better still, the researcher should not know who has been given the drug and who has been given the placebo (this is known as a **double-blind trial**). If the placebo drug has an effect then we know that it is because of psychological factors: the effect represents how much improvement (or deterioration) you would get simply from the effect of someone believing they are taking a helpful medication. You might think that just believing you're taking a drug that will help you will not have a strong effect, but, in fact, placebo effects can be very powerful.

Quick test

1. How do neurons communicate?

2. What are the main brain structures that are important in clinical psychology?

3. How do drug therapies work?

4. What is a placebo treatment and why is it important?

Section 5

End of chapter assessment

Questions

1. How would a psychodynamic therapist explain and treat mental illness?

2. How would a behaviour therapist explain and treat mental illness?

3. How would a cognitive therapist explain and treat mental illness?

4. Are cognitive and behavioural approaches to psychopathology incompatible?

5. What are the important systems in the brain?

6. How does the biological model try to explain psychological problems?

Section 6

Further reading

Davey, G. C. L. and Field, A. P. (in press). Learning and Conditioning. To appear in P. McGhee (Ed.), *Introduction to Contemporary Psychology*. Palgrave. (This is a basic introduction to learning theory.)

Eysenck, H. J. (1985). *Decline and Fall of the Freudian Empire*. London: Penguin.

Rachman, S. J. (1997). The evolution of cognitive behaviour therapy. In D. M. Clark and C. G. Fairburn (Eds.), *Science and Practice of Cognitive Behaviour Therapy*. Oxford: Oxford University Press (pp. 3–26).

Chapter 3
Specific phobias

Chapter summary

This chapter looks at specific phobias and we'll begin by looking at how clinicians diagnose specific phobias. Next, we shall see the extent to which learning processes (conditioning) can contribute to fears by looking at both traditional and contemporary learning models. We shall see that although these models have provided a very useful basis for treatment, they cannot account for curious findings such as that there are common themes found in phobic individuals (such as snakes and spiders). This leads us to consider the possibility that individuals might be predisposed to learn to fear certain stimuli and situations. However, even this 'preparedness' hypothesis has some limitations and so we consider ways in which individuals with phobias might think differently from people without phobias. The chapter concludes by explaining how specific phobias are treated.

Assessment targets

After reading this chapter you should be able to:

Target 1: Explain the key diagnostic criteria for specific phobia. Question 1 at the end of this chapter tests you on this.

Target 2: Explain how phobias are learnt, and know the limitations of this explanation. Question 2 at the end of this chapter tests you on this.

Target 3: Explain preparedness theory and be aware of its limitations. Question 3 at the end of this chapter tests you on this.

Target 4: Explain what is meant by a cognitive bias and show how they contribute to specific phobias. Question 4 at the end of this chapter tests you on this.

Target 5: Explain how specific phobias are treated and relate the therapy back to the theories on which it is based. Question 5 at the end of this chapter tests you on this.

Section 1

What is a specific phobia?

This section will look at how clinical psychologists diagnose simple phobias and explore some of the problems with the diagnostic criteria. We saw in Chapter 1 that classification of psychological disorders is very important for both research and treatment. However we also looked at how the process of classification can be very difficult. The things to think about within this section relate back to Chapter 1: do you think the classification of simple phobias produces mutually exclusive groups of people? As you read the following chapters on anxiety disorders (Chapters 3–6), think about the similarities and differences in diagnosis and think about whether a person might be diagnosed as having different disorders by different clinicians!

I will start by looking at what a phobia is by exploring some common phobias that you might have come across. I'll then describe the *DSM-IV* criteria for simple phobia, and then I'll try to look at some of the problems with the diagnostic criteria.

Diagnosis of specific phobias

There are actually three forms of phobia: **simple** or **specific phobia**, **social phobia** and **agoraphobia** (see Chapter 4). Specific phobias are unique within this group because they are confined to a specific object or situation. Most of us have come across some form of phobia in our lives; for example, lots of you might have, or know people with, mild forms of arachnophobia (fear of spiders), ophidiophobia (snakes) or acrophobia (heights). There are some other relatively common phobias such as nosophobia (injury/illness) and thanato-phobia (death), but there are more unusual ones too; in fact, it's possible to acquire a phobia of virtually anything.

CRUCIAL CONCEPT

What makes a phobia different from a fear? One difference is probably that fears are typically rational. For example, it is perfectly reasonable to experience excessive fear when confronted by a very hungry looking tiger because the chances are it will eat you. However, it's perhaps less reasonable to be paralysed with fear when confronted with a piece of polystyrene. A second difference is avoidance: people with a phobia will try their best to avoid situations in which they might come across the thing of which they're scared.

CRUCIAL DIAGNOSIS

The *Diagnostic and Statistical Manual of Mental Disorders (DSM-IV)* **characterises specific phobias as follows:**

A. A marked and persistent fear that is excessive or unreasonable, cued by the presence or anticipation of a specific object or situation.
B. Exposure to the phobic stimulus almost invariably provokes an immediate anxiety response.
C. The person recognises that the fear is excessive or unreasonable.
D. The phobic situation is avoided or else endured with intense distress.
E. The avoidance, anxious anticipation, or distress in the feared situation interferes significantly with the person's normal routine, occupation (or academic) functioning, or social activities or relationships, or there is marked distress about having the phobia.
F. In under-18s there must be a minimum duration of six months.
G. The symptoms are not better accounted for by another diagnosis.

The key parts of these diagnostic criteria are that the fear must be unreasonable compared to the threat posed to the person and the person should be aware that their fear is unreasonable. Also, the stimulus that evokes the fear is avoided or tolerated with intense distress (so, your average spider phobic will leave the room if they see a spider).

CRUCIAL TIP

A couple of very important things that occur in many different diagnostic criteria are that **the symptoms must not be explained better by another diagnosis**, and that **the disorder interferes substantially with everyday life**. The first is a safeguard that most diagnostic criteria have to ensure that the clinician seeks alternative explanations for the symptoms and only makes a firm diagnosis when he or she is convinced that it is the one that best fits the symptoms. It is also important that a disorder interferes with everyday functioning, because if the patient does not find the disorder debilitating there is probably no benefit from treatment. Look through the remaining chapters of this book and see how often these two criteria appear for the diagnosis of other disorders.

The good aspects of these diagnostic criteria are that they clearly separate specific phobias from other types of phobias such as social phobia because they state that anxiety must be immediately caused by a specific object or situation. You'll see in Chapters 4 and 5 that other forms of anxiety cannot be traced to a single object or situation. The bad aspects of these criteria are that in some sense they are very vague in the terms that they use. For example, what constitutes an unreasonable or excessive fear? Most of us might agree that running away screaming from a peanut is an excessive and unreasonable response, because even though to someone with a nut allergy the peanut poses a fatal threat, most peanuts don't jump up into people's mouths of their own free will! However, is a fear of spiders unreasonable, given that some of them can actually kill you? Also, what do we mean by interfering with daily function? For example, is it enough to occasionally have to sleep in another room when you spot a spider crawling across your bedroom floor, or should we be looking for people who spend hours checking every corner of the room before they go to bed?

CRUCIAL CASE STUDY

EF is a middle-aged housewife who is extremely scared of crane flies (those flying daddy-long-legs that start flocking through the UK air every August-September). She knows that crane flies can't hurt her, but they scare her anyway. During crane fly season EF keeps all of the windows in her house closed for fear that a crane fly might find its way into the house. When leaving the house she traps herself in her porch, her husband then has to check outside for crane flies. Once he gives the all clear, she runs, flapping a fly swatter around her head, to the waiting car (the door of which is opened with clinical precision so as to stop any particularly cunning crane flies from entering the car when no one is looking). Think of the diagnostic criteria for specific phobia, do you think EF has a specific phobia?

Quick test

1. What are the key features of a specific phobia?
2. What is the difference between a fear and a phobia?

Section 2

Do we learn to be scared?

There are several possible ways in which people could acquire phobias. At a fundamental level, we can examine nearly any clinical disorder in terms of nature or nurture: are we born with the disorder, or do we learn it through interacting with our environment? This section will look at the nurture side of this debate by examining the evidence that fears and phobias can be learnt.

Learning to fear

Children experience general patterns of normative fear throughout their development (see Field & Davey, 2001). These fears often appear and disappear spontaneously and follow a predictable course. A wealth of research (e.g. Muris, Merckelbach, & Collaris, 1997; Muris, Merckelbach, Meesters and Van Lier, 1997; Ollendick & King, 1991; Silverman & Nelles, 1989; Campbell, 1986; Bauer, 1976) suggests that normal fears follow a distinctive developmental course: during infancy children tend to fear stimuli within their immediate environment (e.g. loud noises, objects and separation from a caretaker, water and heights); as they get older (4–8 years old) children typically start to fear ghosts and animals; once they reach pre-adolescence they become more likely to fear self-injury, and in early adolescence they fear social situations and criticism. These fears are not phobias, however, just a normal part of development. However, this developmental pattern does correspond to the retrospectively reported age of onset of related adult phobias (see Field & Davey, 2001). For example, people with height and water phobia claim to have always had their fear (Menzies and Clarke, 1993a,b) while the mean ages of onset of animal, blood-injection, and social phobias are 7, 9 and 15–20 years respectively (Öst, 1987). However, the correspondence between the developmental pattern of normal fears and the onset ages of adult phobias does not mean that normative fears will necessarily develop into phobias, partly it will depend on experience. We saw in Chapter 2 that one way in which people learn is through conditioning (see Chapter 2 and Davey & Field, in press).

CRUCIAL STUDY

In the early 1900s Watson and Rayner (1920) conducted a now legendary experiment that showed that a nine-month old child, Albert B (or 'Little Albert' as he became known), could be conditioned to fear a white rat. Albert was pre-tested to ensure that he was not initially fearful of the rat (which acted as a predictor, or CS), and that he was naturally fearful of a loud noise made by banging a claw hammer on an iron bar (which acted as an aversive outcome, or UCS). Albert was placed in a room with the rat and every time he approached or touched the rat, Watson scared Albert by hitting the iron bar. After several pairings of the rat with the loud noise, Albert began to cry whenever he saw the rat (remember that initially Albert had not been scared of the rat). The implication from this experiment was that excessive and persistent fear (i.e. a phobia) could be acquired through experiencing any innocuous stimulus in temporal proximity to some fear-inducing or traumatic event.

The learning model of fear suggests that people acquire fear of a stimulus simply because they have associated it with a negative or traumatic outcome. Mowrer (1960) extended this idea to a two-stage theory. In the first stage a person learns to associate a stimulus with an aversive outcome resulting in a learnt fear response. In the second stage the person learns that by avoiding the stimulus that evokes fear, they can reduce their fear (which acts as an incentive for further avoidance). This theory accounts for the persistent avoidance behaviour that phobics display. The learning theory operates on a purely behavioural level: phobias are just learnt responses that are relatively independent of a person's thoughts (refer back to Chapter 2). It follows from this that to treat a phobia all you would need to do is remove the learnt response (see Section 5).

More recent work has verified that things can become feared simply through association with trauma; for example, Dollinger, O'Donnell and Staley (1984) found that children surviving a severe lightning-strike showed more numerous and intense fears of thunder-storms, lightning and tornadoes than control children. Similarly, Yule, Udwin and Murdoch (1990) found that teenage survivors of a sinking cruise ship showed an excess of fears relating to ships, water travel, swimming and water, and even other modes of transport, than their peers. Both of these studies suggest that a single traumatic event can lead to intense fears of objects related to the trauma.

The learning model is good because it demonstrates how any stimulus could come to be fear-evoking (if you're a child having your first taste of cabbage when a tornado hits your house you could develop an irrational fear of cabbage). However, Rachman (1977) pointed out that there are several important things that the simple learning model can't explain. First, not all phobics can remember experiencing a traumatic experience at the onset of their phobia (I mentioned earlier that height and water phobics, for example, claim to have always had their fear). Although this alone is not compelling evidence against conditioning because memories can become biased or forgotten over time, it is true that not all people who experience a traumatic event go on to develop a phobia. For example, not all people who experience pain or a traumatic event whilst at the dentist go on to acquire a phobia (Lautch, 1971) and not all fliers who experience a traumatic flying accident develop a fear of flying (Aitken, Lister & Main, 1981). Finally, based on learning we would expect that all stimuli are equally likely to acquire fear-evoking properties, and yet there is an uneven distribution of phobias. Phobias of spiders, snakes, dogs, heights, water, death, thunder, and fire are much more prevalent than phobias of hammers, guns, knives, and electrical outlets yet the latter group of stimuli seem to have a high likelihood of being associated with pain and trauma (see Field & Davey, 2001 for more details of the criticisms of the learning model).

Outcome expectancies

However, the learning model can be saved through recent advances in our understanding of human conditioning processes. For example, Davey (1997) has suggested that the likelihood of whether an association is made between a stimulus and a traumatic outcome depends upon a person's expectations prior to the learning episode. For example, if we expect something bad to happen when we see a spider, and something bad does indeed happen, then we're more likely to make the connection between spiders and trauma than if we'd previously expected something good to happen when we see a spider. These are called **outcome expectancies**.

CRUCIAL CONCEPT

Vicarious learning (also known as **observational learning** or **modelling**) is learning something through watching someone else. So we might learn that mice are scary because we've seen our mother standing on a chair screaming as a mouse runs around the floor!

What is likely to influence our expectancies? According to Rachman's (1977, 1991) model there are two types of experience other than direct learning that contribute to adult phobia:

- learning through observing others (vicarious learning); and
- the transmission of negative information.

It appears that there is evidence that mothers' reactions to stimuli can increase the likelihood of their children developing anxiety (Muris, Steerneman, Merckelbach, & Meesters, 1996) and that laboratory-reared rhesus monkeys can learn to fear snakes just by watching videos of wild monkeys responding anxiously towards a snake (Mineka, Davidson, Cook, & Weir, 1984). Fear information too seems to have some effect on fear beliefs: Field, Argyris & Knowles (2001) demonstrated that fear information (especially from adults) about unknown animals increased children's fear beliefs about those animals and will make children reluctant to touch those animals (Field & Lawson, 2002).

We also know that events in the past – and especially the consequences of an event – can subsequently be revalued (see crucial case study below). Davey (1997) suggests that this explains why not all phobics remember a traumatic experience.

CRUCIAL CASE STUDY

Client H.B. was a severe spider phobic. She had lived in Rio de Janeiro in Brazil during her childhood and once, at the age of 10 years, when she woke during the night a large tropical spider walked over her face. Although calm at the time (she did not have a traumatic experience), when she told her parents about what had happened the next morning, they expressed extreme concern. From that moment on, H.B. was extremely frightened of spiders and exhibited severe phobic behaviour (from Davey, de Jong & Tallis, 1993). This example demonstrates how an initially non-traumatic event came to evoke anxiety because its consequences were revalued (in this case by the parents expressing concern at how dangerous the spider might have been).

Quick test

1. How can specific phobias be explained in terms of learning?

2. What are the main shortcomings of the learning theory of specific phobias?

Section 3

Are we born to fear?

The fact that phobias of spiders, snakes, dogs, heights, water, death, thunder, and fire are much more prevalent than phobias of modern threats to safety such as hammers, guns, knives and electrical outlets suggests that humans might be hard-wired to acquire certain kinds of fears. This section looks at the evidence that we are born to fear certain stimuli and situations.

Preparedness theory

--- CRUCIAL CONCEPT ---

Preparedness is the idea that we are born to acquire fears of certain stimuli faster than others because these stimuli were a threat to our ancient ancestors.

If we are born with a 'hard-wired' fear of certain stimuli or situations then we might expect two things:

- children would be scared of certain things from birth; and
- there should be common themes in what people fear.

We saw in the previous section that there are common themes in what people fear, and we also saw that children go through a fairly rigid developmental pattern of normal fears. In addition, Menzies and Clarke (1993a, b) suggest that water and height phobics do indeed report having been scared for as long as they can remember. Two explanations have been put forward:

- **preparedness theory** (Seligman, 1971); and
- **non-associative explanations** (Poulton & Menzies, 2002).

Non-associative theories hinge on the idea that people are born with a tendency to fear certain stimuli that were in some way dangerous or lethal to our ancient ancestors. So because our 'caveman' ancestors were under threat from certain animals (e.g. snakes) or situations (heights, water, fire) we have evolved a predisposition to be wary of these stimuli (these stimuli are known as **fear-relevant**). The rationale is that if someone fears a stimulus they are likely to avoid it, so the scared caveman would have avoided potentially lethal situations and survived to pass on his 'scared' genes. Fear releases various chemicals (like adrenalin) that help us deal with the fear-evoking situation (it helps us defend ourselves or, in my case, run away!). Therefore, we evolved this tendency to fear certain threats because any of our ancestors who had not been wary of these stimuli would have been likely to have been killed and not reproduce.

Seligman's preparedness theory differs only in that he suggested that rather than being born wary of certain stimuli, we were born with a tendency to **learn** to fear certain stimuli that were dangerous or lethal to our pretechnological ancestors.

--- CRUCIAL TIP ---

Many students incorrectly think that preparedness theory means that people are born with phobias. However, Seligman didn't suggest that we are born with a fear of certain stimuli, but that we are born with a **predisposition to learn to fear** these stimuli more quickly. So, should we have a negative experience with say a snake, we are more likely to learn a phobic response than if we have a negative experience with, say, a knife. The idea that we are actually born with an innate tendency to fear certain stimuli is not preparedness, but is the 'non-associative' account of fear acquisition (Poulton & Menzies, 2002).

Preparedness provides a very elegant explanation of why certain phobias are more common (i.e. snakes, spiders, insects, heights, water, fire, thunder, open spaces). It also doesn't exclude the possibility that people can develop unusual phobias (e.g. phobia of cardboard) because the theory merely says that we learn to fear certain stimuli more quickly. Finally, preparedness can also explain some irrational fears. For example, spider phobia is very prominent in the UK and yet there are no species of spider in the UK that can do you even the slightest amount of harm. (In fact, only about six of the 50,000 types of spiders in the world are known to be poisonous.) Preparedness would explain this by suggesting that although spiders in the UK are not currently a threat, there might have been threatening spiders lurking around in our ancestral past.

However, is preparedness a realistic theory? For one thing, did these stimuli really threaten our caveman ancestors? Although it's certainly true that our ancestors came from far and wide, there are remarkably few spiders on the planet that can actually kill humans. On a daily basis, the average caveman probably had more to fear from the ancestors of cats and woolly mammoths than he did from the average spider. So why did we acquire a predisposition to spiders and not to other animals such as tigers and elephants (elephant and woolly-mammoth phobias are rare!)? One answer is that we do have a predisposition to fear tigers and the like, but because we have little or no contact with them the predisposition is never put to use. However, equally true is that our contact with spiders is usually non-threatening (unless you live in Sydney and annoy a funnelweb) so why don't we learn not to fear them?

There is also a theoretical problem with making statements about evolutionary processes: in the absence of a time machine, we can never know what posed a threat to our ancestors. Although it's appealing to think that a natural disposition to fear would have helped our ancestors to survive and pass on their genes we can't know that this actually happened. If our ancestors had been that prone to fear then rather than run away or fight they might just have passed out (you'll see in Chapter 4 that if you have a trigger-happy fight-or-flight response you tend to get panic attacks and pass out). The key point is that it is dangerous to speculate about what evolutionary pressures were placed upon our ancestors!

Quick test

1. What is the basic idea behind preparedness and non-associative accounts of fear acquisition?

2. What is the difference between preparedness theory and non-associative explanations of fear?

Section 4

Do we think ourselves into being scared?

The learning and preparedness/non-associative models largely ignore the phobic's thoughts. Another explanation of phobias is that some people actually think differently about threats in their environment. They become scared of certain stimuli or situations simply because they perceive the world in a different way. This section looks at some of what we know about the cognitions in people who have specific phobias. There is an accumulation of evidence for the role of cognitive factors in anxiety generally, so when reading this section you should also look at the corresponding sections in the chapters on social phobia, generalised anxiety disorder and depression.

Cognitive theories of specific phobias

Cognitive theories are based on the idea that phobias are caused by **cognitive biases** or **maladaptive thinking**. The learning explanations in Section 2 pretty much ignored thoughts and relied instead on fear responses being learnt at a relatively reflexive level. Therefore, to treat the phobia you simply treat the learnt behaviour. Cognitive theories are really the opposite in that they assume that cognitive biases drive the phobia and cause the fear response (refer back to Chapter 2). Therefore, if you treat the cognitions, the behaviour will vanish.

Phobic people do seem to attend to threat-relevant material more than non-phobic people: they show a bias towards material related to their fear. Öhman & Soares (1994) found that snake phobics exhibited a fear response to pictures of snakes that were masked (hidden) by another stimulus (so the snake could not be consciously perceived), non-phobics did not exhibit fear. The emotional stroop task (see Chapter 2) can be adapted so that participants have to name the colour of words when some words are threat-relevant (e.g. fangs, hairy and crawl to a spider-phobic) and others are threat irrelevant (e.g. chair, spoon). Williams, Mathews & MacLeod (1996) reviewed the evidence from this kind of task and found that while anxious people take longer to process threat-relevant words than non-threatening words, for controls there is no difference. This means that anxious people are attending to threatening words longer than controls.

Davey (1995) has also suggested that rumination (see Chapter 2) can lead to the enhancement of self-reported anxiety in phobic people. For example, repeatedly thinking about what 'might have happened' after a car accident makes you more anxious than if you just put the car accident out of your mind completely. The implication is that thoughts can enhance anxiety.

The problem with the cognitive approach is that it doesn't explain why some people have these maladaptive thoughts and others don't. It's a chicken-egg situation: does the disorder come from the thoughts or do the thoughts come as a result of the disorder? It is possible that mental disorders are learnt but that cognitive biases act to maintain or exacerbate the feelings of anxiety. As it turns out, there is little evidence that purely addressing cognitions is good therapy for specific phobias (in which sufferers fully acknowledge the irrationality of their thoughts). Therefore, treating thoughts does not always lead to a change in behaviour.

Quick test

What is the basic idea behind cognitive explanations of specific phobias?

Section 5

How are specific phobias treated?

We've had a look at various theories of how phobias develop. The final part of this chapter examines how these theories are put into practice in therapeutic settings. In reality, modern therapy typically tries to change both learnt responses (as described in Section 2) and cognitive biases (as described in Section 4). This type of therapy is called **cognitive behaviour therapy**, or **CBT** for short. Cognitive behaviour therapy blends exposure to the fear-evoking situation with cognitive techniques to help 'cope' with the situation.

How therapy works

The treatment of specific phobias has changed relatively little since Wolpe (1958, 1961, 1962) pioneered therapies aimed at changing learnt fear responses through exposure to the fear-evoking stimulus (see Chapter 2). There are some general principles that can be applied to treatment of different disorders.

- The first step in any behavioural treatment is to establish the precise nature of the phobia and its suitability for treatment (Butler, 1989). A therapist carries out a **functional analysis** to establish whether the anxiety is restricted to certain environments or times (**settings**), whether any particular events have to occur before the phobic behaviour is displayed and if so if they are specific events or a range of events (**triggers**), identify what other events precede the behaviour (**antecedent events**) and finally identify what meaningful outcome of behaviour there was for the client (**results**). Patients and clinicians are rarely aware of all of the important events and so data must be collected over a period of time through patient diaries or interviews with a third party. Maintenance factors should be identified along with secondary gains (things that reinforce anxious behaviour such as people giving you comfort or sympathy). It is crucial to get as full a picture as possible and not to interpret the data and jump to false hypotheses about the causes of the disorder.

- Once eliciting factors have been identified, the therapist should collaborate with the client to establish the **goals of therapy**. The general goal of therapy for phobics is often self-evident (i.e. to stop being afraid) but it is very important that the clinician discusses the precise goals with the client to avoid any potential confusion. For example, the clinician should always make the client aware that spontaneous recurrence of symptoms is to be expected.

- Having established the maintenance factors and set up mutually agreeable goals, the next stage is to **measure the phobia** using easy and sensitive measures that reflect the client's individual concerns. Measures are vital to assess the progress of a therapeutic technique; it is necessary to compare the patient's behaviour against an initial baseline measure throughout therapy to monitor the effects of any intervention. As the therapist introduces new techniques they look at the effect it has on behaviour to see whether or not it was effective.

There are several ways to measure phobia severity. One way is to use a graded hierarchy in which the patient thinks of several situations from a minimal fear situation (e.g. a small garden spider standing still several meters away from the patient) to a maximum fear intensity situation (e.g. a huge, black, hairy spider with visible fangs crawling across the patient's face). The patient then ranks these situations and rates the anxiety and avoidance that each situation would provoke (on a scale of 1–10 or 1–100). Often it is easier for the patient to think of extreme examples and then think of items that lie in between the two extremes.

Hierarchies are often a lot more difficult to construct than they first appear because fears may be difficult to grade into small steps (e.g. fear of flying). In addition, patients often avoid situations and yet are totally unaware that they are doing so or are oblivious to the precise nature of their phobia (a spider phobic may not be scared of spiders *per se*, it may specifically be their movement). If they find constructing a hierarchy difficult it may be useful for the patient to read, talk or write about their phobia and watch relevant films in order to gain inspiration about the sorts of situations they find most and least anxiety evoking.

Behavioural tests can also be used in which clients do something that they would normally avoid (e.g. watching a house spider crawling around a bowl) and rate their anxiety at the time. This is especially useful when the patient has an extensive pattern of avoidance and is merely guessing about the anxiety experienced. Standardised questionnaires, which measure specific phobic anxiety, such as the Fear Questionnaire and the Fear Survey Schedule, can be used also.

Treatment

The actual treatment procedure chosen will depend on a detailed assessment of aetiology. However specific phobias are typically treated using some form of **exposure**. In its crudest form, **flooding**, the patient is exposed to the fear-evoking stimulus for a long period of time: although anxiety initially increases it eventually peaks and then subsides. As such, the patient eventually learns to be calm in the presence of their feared stimulus. However, the success of this technique seems to depend upon the length of exposure: patients must be exposed long enough for their fear to subside.

Although modern therapies are still based on exposure, they are slightly more refined; a traditional treatment for specific phobia is **systematic desensitisation** (Wolpe, 1961). During the sessions the patient is taught how to relax and is asked to practise the relaxation techniques at home until they can reach a certain degree of relaxation. In the therapy itself the patient is asked to relax and told to signal by raising his or her index finger if (s)he feels at all anxious or disturbed during the procedure. At first a neutral scene is imagined before moving on to the lowest situation in the graded hierarchy generated earlier. Subsequent sessions begin with the patient imagining the highest situation in the hierarchy that could be imagined without fear at the previous session before moving on to the next situation in the hierarchy. If at any time the patient looks anxious or indicates anxiety, they are given a relaxing scenario to imagine. The sessions are ended when the highest situation in the graded hierarchy can be imagined without anxiety.

Nowadays exposure is usually conducted using behavioural tasks extracted from the hierarchy as well as, or instead of, imaginal exposure. The critical guidelines for exposure are that it should repeated, graduated and prolonged with tasks being specified and agreed upon in advance (Butler, 1985). However, the unforeseeable nature of phobic stimuli can pose a problem (e.g. how do you know when you are going to come across a spider?). These unpredictabilities interfere with the systematic repetition and graduation of exposure episodes. To overcome this problem therapists sometimes get patients to practise an array of tasks encompassing a range of difficulty in the same week as opposed to stringently moving up the hierarchy.

The administration of exposure is not just restricted to the clinical session – patients are empowered with the ability to cope with their phobic stimuli alone. An important step towards this is to set homework for the client. Although initial stages of exposure should be undertaken with the clinician until such a time that the patient feels confident enough to do homework on his/her own, many of the behavioural tasks set by the clinician can be undertaken outside of the clinical setting. The patient should be encouraged to undertake home-based treatment often with a relative or friend who has been informed, in detail, about the treatment.

How successful is therapy?

The reason therapies for simple phobias have changed relatively little since the exposure-based therapies of the 1960s is because evidence suggests that they are very effective. In 1993 the American Psychological Association set up a task force whose aim was to promote and disseminate effective clinical practices for different disorders. Based on published experimental clinical trials and well-controlled case studies this task force accumulated evidence about which therapies were effective for which disorders (APA, 1993). They concluded that simple exposure and systematic desensitisation were both effective treatments for simple phobias (see also Marks, 1987). In addition, this effectiveness cannot be attributed to non-specific factors of therapy (Kazdin & Wilcoxin, 1976; Gelder et al., 1973). Therapy can also have generalisable effects such as improvements in relationships and increased self confidence, and it has been noted that exposure has cognitive as well as behavioural effects (Butler, 1989). Stern and Marks (1973) concluded that anxiety levels during exposure have little effect on the outcome but in general prolonged exposure is more effective than brief exposure. As such, exposure per se is not predictive of outcome but duration of exposure can be (in general). Look at Chapters 4-6 to see how successful this form of therapy is for other anxiety disorders.

Quick test

1. What is a functional analysis and why is it important?

2. What is a graded hierarchy and how is it used in systematic desensitisation?

3. Is cognitive behaviour therapy for specific phobias successful?

Section 6

End of chapter assessment

Questions

1. What is a specific phobia?

2. How has learning theory informed the treatment of phobias?

3. Are learning theories and preparedness incompatible explanations of specific phobias?

4. Are phobias the result of maladaptive cognitions?

5. Does the success of exposure therapy mean that cognitions are not important in specific phobias?

Section 7

Further reading

Butler, G. (1989). Phobic disorders. In K. Hawton, P.M. Salkovskis, J. Kirk and D.M. Clark (Eds.), *Cognitive Behaviour Therapy for Psychiatric Problems: A Practical Guide.* Oxford: Oxford University Press. (This is, in my view, the clearest account of how therapy for specific phobias is put into place.)

Davey, G. C. L. (Ed.) (1997). *Phobias: A handbook of theory, research and treatment.* Chichester: Wiley. (This book is quite high level but really does tell you everything you need to know about phobias.)

Field, A. P. & Davey, G. C. L. (2001). Conditioning models of childhood anxiety. In W. K. Silverman, & P. A. Treffers (Eds.) *Anxiety Disorders in Children and Adolescents: Research, Assessment and Intervention* (pp. 187–211). Cambridge: Cambridge University Press. (This chapter goes into more detail about how learning models can be used to explain the development of fears and phobias.)

Chapter 4
Panic disorder and social phobia

Chapter summary

This chapter progresses our understanding of anxiety disorders by looking at two closely related disorders: **panic disorder** and **social phobia** (also called **social anxiety disorder**). First, we will look at how clinicians diagnose these disorders before considering explanations of them. We look at the three most influential explanations of panic disorder: biological, learning and cognitive explanations. You will see that biological explanations are based on the idea that the fight-or-flight mechanism is oversensitive in people with panic disorder, learning models are based on the idea that somatic symptoms are conditioned to inflated states of anxiety, and cognitive models describe the cognitive processes involved in a panic attack. Next we look at explanations of social phobia, which have focused on cognitions and how they lead social phobics to interpret social situations in a negative way. Finally, we'll find out how panic and social phobias are treated using cognitive and behavioural techniques.

Assessment targets

After reading this chapter you should be able to:

Target 1: Explain the key diagnostic criteria for social phobia and panic. Questions 1 and 2 at the end of the chapter test you on this.

Target 2: Explain the similarities and differences between models of panic and social phobia. Question 3 at the end of the chapter tests you on this.

Target 3: Explain biological theories of panic and be aware of their limitations. Question 4 at the end of the chapter tests you on this.

Target 4: Explain what cognitive biases contribute to social phobia and panic. Question 5 at the end of the chapter tests you on this.

Target 5: Understand how social phobia and panic are treated and relate the therapeutic techniques back to the theories on which they are based. Question 6 at the end of the chapter tests you on this.

Section 1

How are social phobia and panic different?

This section will look at the differences between how clinical psychologists diagnose social phobia and panic and explore some of the problems with the diagnostic criteria. As I've mentioned in previous chapters (1 and 3) it is very important for research and treatment that psychological disorders are accurately diagnosed, but the process of classification can be very difficult. While reading this section, ask yourself whether panic and social phobia should be thought of as different disorders, and whether panic seems distinct from the specific phobias described in Chapter 3.

I will start by looking at the history of panic and social phobia before describing their respective *DSM-IV* criteria and some of the problems with them.

A historical background

In early versions of *DSM*, panic and social phobia were treated as a single disorder. In fact, it was only really the discovery that social phobia with panic attacks responded to different drugs than phobia without panic attacks by Klein (1964) that led to them being distinguished in 1980. Even though they respond to different drugs, theoretical models and treatments of the two disorders have substantial overlap, which is why I'll consider these syndromes together. Panic disorder has an approximate lifetime prevalence of 2% in men and 5% in women and the typical age of onset is late adolescence to mid-30s. Around 92% of sufferers experience attacks for at least one year and the disorder is often associated with other anxiety disorders, depression, substance use and personality disorders. Social phobia affects around 8% of the population and typically begins during adolescence (Öst, 1987) and is associated with depression and panic.

Diagnosis of panic

According to *DSM-IV*, a panic attack is a discrete period in which there is a sudden onset of intense apprehension, fearfulness, or terror associated with at least four symptoms including: breathlessness, palpitations, dizziness, trembling, nausea, feelings of choking, de-realisation, chest pain, paresthesia (a sensation of pricking, tingling, or creeping on the skin that seemingly has no cause), and a fear of going crazy, losing control or dying (APA, 1994). This sort of experience is common in the majority of anxiety disorders. In fact most of us will have experienced a panic attack like this at some point in our lives. Anywhere between about 7–40% of people experience occasional unexpected panic attacks especially during periods of intense stress (e.g. King, Gullone & Tonge, 1993). However, these attacks remain only an inconvenience, do not threaten normal activities, and remain isolated to the stressful period. So what distinguishes these people from those with panic disorder?

CRUCIAL DIAGNOSIS

The *Diagnostic and Statistical Manual of Mental Disorders* (*DSM-IV*) characterises panic as follows:

A. Recurrent unexpected panic attacks: attacks must be uncued (i.e. they cannot be attributed to a specific event or stimulus) otherwise they form part of a phobia.

B. At least one of the attacks has been followed by one month of
 • persistent concern about the attack;
 • worry about the implications or consequences of the attack;
 • a significant change in behaviour due to the attacks.

C. Absence/presence of agoraphobia: panic can be diagnosed with or without agoraphobia. Patients diagnosed as having panic with agoraphobia can identify certain situations that are more likely to trigger an attack and will avoid those situations. Those diagnosed as having panic disorder without agoraphobia can identify no such circumstances (so attacks truly seem to occur randomly).

D. Panic attacks should not be due to substances or a medical condition.

E. Panic attacks should not be better explained by another diagnosis.

The key parts of these diagnostic criteria are that the panic attacks should be uncued, that is, the person cannot identify a particular stimulus or situation that causes them to panic. Like specific phobias (see Chapter 3) the panic attacks must be recurrent, cause distress (concern and worry about the attacks) and interfere with everyday life (the person changes their behaviour because of the attacks). Another similarity with other diagnostic criteria is that it must not be better explained by an alternative diagnosis. This issue comes back to the point that diagnostic criteria should result in mutually exclusive groups of people (see Chapter 1). For example, if the panic is triggered by a specific stimulus (such as a clinical psychology exam), then it is better explained as a specific phobia (because a particular event triggers it) in which panic is triggered by specific stimuli (e.g. spiders), or there could be medical conditions that cause the panic attacks.

CRUCIAL TIP

As we've seen, panic can be diagnosed with or without agoraphobia. Most people think of agoraphobia as being a fear of open spaces (its literal translation is 'fear of the market place'), however, this is not true. In fact, agoraphobics are terrified of a variety of public situations including walking along the street, travelling on public transport, and visiting shops and shopping malls. When confronted with these situations, sufferers experience severe panic attacks that, over time, usually result in the person remaining at home or going out only if a close relative or friend remains close by at all times. Although commonly thought to be a syndrome of 'mature housewives', the male to female ratio in studies using *DSM* criteria is in the region of 1:2. In panic without agoraphobia, panic attacks appear to the sufferer to occur randomly, whereas in panic with agoraphobia the sufferer is aware of the situations that trigger the feelings of panic.

The good aspects of these diagnostic criteria are that they clearly separate panic from specific phobias because they state that panic must not be cued by a specific object or situation. These criteria also attempt to ensure that the panic attacks occur over a prolonged period and result in a change of behaviour to exclude the large number of people who experience occasional attacks. However, the downside again is that the criteria are couched in vague terms. For example, how can 'persistent concern' be quantified? Does it mean worrying about the panic attack for a minute a day for a week, or should the person have weeks of sleepless nights thinking about the catastrophic implications of their attacks? Of course, a certain degree of flexibility in the criteria is a good thing because it allows trained clinicians to use their experience to guide diagnosis.

CRUCIAL CASE STUDY

Jane, 55, vividly remembered having her first panic attack when she was in her teens. Since then she frequently feels something happen to her body 'out of the blue'; in particular she notes her heart beating fast, her palms and brow sweating, feeling short of breath and dizzy. These attacks often last over five minutes and occur at least five times a week. At the time she feels like something terrible is happening inside her body and is terrified that she will become out of control, at best, or die at worst. On one occasion she experienced panic when on a busy train, and she no longer uses the London Underground because she fears the same pattern of events.

Diagnosis of social phobia

Social phobia differs from panic in that specific types of situations cue anxiety. Most sufferers of social phobia can interact comfortably with certain people (such as family members) but experience extreme anxiety in a variety of other situations. Although social phobics often believe that others interpret their social behaviour as indicative of intense anxiety, they often will not apply this rule of thumb when interpreting others' behaviour towards them. Social anxiety can be 'generalised', meaning that it is triggered by a wide range of situations, or 'non-generalised', meaning that a more limited set of situations act as triggers. Most of us can relate to feeling anxious in certain social contexts, such as giving a presentation to your psychology seminar group (in fact, despite having given hundreds of lectures I still get extremely nervous before each one), so how does social phobia differ from these normal responses?

CRUCIAL DIAGNOSIS

The *Diagnostic and Statistical Manual of Mental Disorders* (*DSM-IV*) characterises social phobia as follows:

A. A marked and persistent fear of one or more social or performance situations in which the person is exposed to unfamiliar people or possible scrutiny by others.

B. Exposure evokes an immediate reaction.

C. The person realises their fear is irrational.

D. The feared situation is avoided.
   • This avoidance interferes with 'normal' life.

E. For under-18s there should be a minimum duration of six months.

F. The anxiety is not better explained by another diagnosis.

In fact, according to *DSM* there isn't a lot to discriminate normal performance anxiety from social phobia in terms of the actual anxiety experienced. However, most people do not avoid these situations (I can still give my lectures despite my nerves). Exposure to the situation will, in most of us, not enhance our anxiety (you should get calmer), and the variety of experiences that trigger these reactions will be fairly limited in most of us (so, we might get anxious about giving a talk but most of us don't get anxious about going to a pub where we know there will be some unfamiliar people).

As with specific phobias (see Chapter 3), the person has to realise that the fear is irrational. The sufferer has to realise that actually the social situation poses no real threat. So despite my visions of 100 undergraduates storming to the front of the lecture theatre to stab me for being such a terrible lecturer, I realise that this is extremely unlikely to happen: it's very unusual to suffer injury or death from giving a talk (however, it's not unlikely that you might die – of boredom – from listening to one of my talks!). Also, because of the general heightened sensitivity to social evaluation in teenagers, those below the age of 18 need to have had a problem for six months or more and their anxiety should be general and not just limited to anxiety experienced around adults.

Quick test

1. What are the key diagnostic features of panic?
2. What are the key diagnostic features of social phobia?

Section 2

Can we explain panic disorder?

Panic disorder could develop in several ways and as with specific phobias (Chapter 3) the main opposing views are that some people are born with the disorder (or born with something that predisposes them to the disorder), or that, other things being equal, we could all develop the disorder through experience. This section looks at various theories of panic disorder, first by looking at biological explanations, and then looking at behavioural and cognitive factors.

Born to panic

If we were born to panic then that would mean that certain biological mechanisms exist in us all that cause us to have panic attacks; and for such a mechanism to exist we might need to think about whether panic has an adaptive purpose. In fact, one of the most basic survival responses (found in virtually all animals) is the **fight-or-flight** response. The basic idea is that when faced with danger (e.g. a large tiger dressed in a dinner jacket waving a knife and fork) our body does various things to help us out: it increases our blood flow (by increasing heart rate) and metabolism, stops unnecessary activities such as digestion, reduces the production of saliva and mucus to increase the size of the air passages to our lungs, and releases glucose and hormones so that fats are more quickly broken down into protein and sugars (the body's source of energy). The net effect is our body becomes prepared to expend energy either in defence or by running away. If our body didn't do this then when the aforementioned tiger came after us we'd be slower to run away because we'd still be digesting our last meal, we couldn't get energy quick enough and so we'd soon become tired, and the mucus in our airways would prevent us getting sufficient air to keep on running! These responses should be familiar to you – they are what you feel when you are anxious or threatened.

CRUCIAL CONCEPTS

The **autonomic nervous system** (**ANS**) is the system in the body that regulates glands and so-called 'smooth muscles'. Importantly, it controls the adrenal glands, heart, intestines and stomach. This system is kept in balance by two (usually) opposing subsystems:
1. The **sympathetic nervous system** creates physiological arousal when required. For example, it increases heart rate and activates glands to secrete hormones (such as the adrenal gland to produce adrenalin).
2. The **parasympathetic nervous system** inhibits physiological arousal. The parasympathetic nervous system tends to be dominant most of the time and regulates basic functions such as digestion. However, in times of stress or activity the sympathetic nervous system tends to become dominant.

CRUCIAL CONCEPT

The **fight-or-flight** response is a collection of physiological changes that prepare an animal in times of threat or stress. These responses include an increase in heart rate and metabolism, cessation of unnecessary bodily activities, a reduction in saliva and mucus, and increased levels of glucose and certain hormones (e.g. adrenalin).

The autonomic nervous system controls fight-or-flight responses using its two subsystems (see above). Ordinarily, fight-or-flight responses are inhibited by the parasympathetic nervous system unless some external threat comes along at which point the sympathetic nervous system leaps into action. The theories that suggest that certain people are born to panic are all based to some extent on the failure of certain people to regulate their fight-or-flight response. For example, Rapee, Brown, Anthony and Barlow (1992) found that if panic disorder patients purposely hyperventilate, breathe into a paper bag (which increases their intake of carbon dioxide), or inhale carbon dioxide (CO_2) they are much more likely to have a panic attack (around 45–65%) than control participants. Therefore, some have suggested that panic disorder is simply the result of an overactive fight-or-flight response (McNally, 1990). Gorman, Liebowitz, Fyer, Fyer & Klein (1986) similarly suggested that the sympathetic and parasympathetic nervous systems are out of balance in panic sufferers (or become easily de-stabilised) resulting in panic attacks.

Klein (1993) noted that all of the processes that induce panic (e.g. hyperventilation, breathing into a paper bag and inhaling CO_2) involve an increase in levels of carbon dioxide to the brain. He therefore proposed the **suffocation false alarm theory**, which suggests that panic sufferers' brains are particularly sensitive to increases in CO_2. Humans breathe oxygen, not carbon dioxide, and Klein suggested that panic sufferers' brains interpret an increase in CO_2 as meaning that they will suffocate, which triggers a full blown fight-or-flight response.

The final few biological theories are based on neurotransmitters (see Chapter 2). We saw in Chapter 2 that the limbic system is the information pathway between the brain stem (which receives signals about bodily functions) and the cortex (where these signals are interpreted). This information pathway relies on noradrenergic neurotransmitters for communication and Reiman et al. (1986) have found increased activity levels of these neurotransmitters (e.g. norepinephrine) in the limbic system of panic patients who were having panic attacks. However, it's difficult to know whether this increased activation caused the panic or was merely a by-product of it. Likewise panic sufferers may have a deficiency in noradrenergic neurotransmitters (e.g. serotonin) in the limbic system, which makes the fight-or-flight response hyperactive (so the threshold for a panic attack is permanently reduced).

Thinking ourselves into a panic

Probably the most influential explanation of panic is Clark's (1986) cognitive model. Clark believed that even though panic attacks appear to be un-cued, there is usually a **trigger stimulus** or stimuli. These stimuli can be either external, like in agoraphobia (e.g. a crowded supermarket), or internal (i.e. thoughts, body sensations, or images). The important thing about these trigger stimuli is that they are perceived as threatening, so they are seen as predictors of impending danger. This is the starting point of Clark's model as shown in Figure 2. This perceived threat creates apprehension, which is associated with a variety of bodily sensations such as an increase in heart rate and sweating. The key to the cycle is that these bodily sensations are then interpreted in a catastrophic way; for example, the increase in heart rate could be seen as indicative of an oncoming heart attack or impending loss of control or insanity. This process of catastrophic misinterpretation increases the perceived threat and, therefore, the apprehension experienced. Now that the apprehension is even greater, the bodily sensations increase again and are again interpreted catastrophically, leading to even greater perceived threat. It's easy to see that this process quickly becomes a vicious circle that culminates in a panic attack.

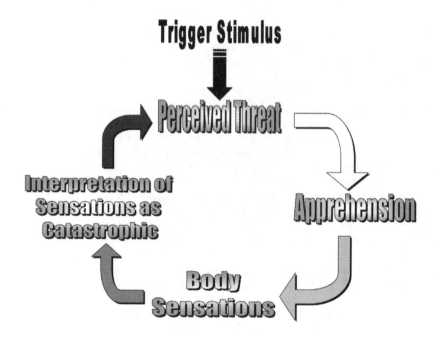

Figure 2: Clark's (1986) model of panic

CRUCIAL CONCEPT

Safety behaviours: these are behaviours in which anxiety sufferers engage because they believe that by engaging in them they will prevent some negative outcome. Typically these behaviours are counter-productive in that they prevent the person from gathering accurate information about the true state of the world and merely reinforce their biased view of reality. An example might be avoiding eye contact to prevent seeing a negative facial expression.

Clark identified two other important mechanisms that are not in Figure 2. First, Clark suggested that once someone has developed the tendency to interpret bodily sensations catastrophically they become hypervigilant and repeatedly scan their bodies for sensations. He called this, **hypervigilance**. This internal focus allows these people to notice sensations that others would not, and interpret them as further evidence of some physical or mental disorder. Second, Clark noticed that like many anxious people, panic sufferers engage in safety behaviours in which they avoid panic-related situations. For example, someone preoccupied with having a heart attack might avoid exercise believing that this helps prevent a heart attack. Of course this behaviour merely prevents the person from discovering that an increased heart rate and skipped beats are perfectly normal sensations.

There is some support for Clark's model in that people with panic disorder (may) misinterpret their bodily sensations as signs of impending physical disaster more than controls. For example, Clark *et al.* (1994) report that successful treatment of panic patients reduces the level of misinterpretation of bodily sensations (but this doesn't tell us whether panic causes misinterpretation or vice versa). Also, thoughts of imminent danger do seem to accompany panic attacks (Beck *et al.*, 1985), and panic disorder patients report more negative cognitions when panic is induced (Yeragani *et al.*, 1988). Recent work has also shown that unexplained physiological arousal leads to panic attacks in panic patients (Leonard, Telch & Harrington, 1999).

One good aspect of this model is that it accounts for both panic triggered by a state of heightened anxiety (i.e. some event unrelated to the panic attack heightens anxiety, or anticipation of a panic attack) and panic that appears to occur randomly. In reality panic attacks are rarely random, they are usually triggered by some event such as standing up quickly or palpitations caused by drinking too much caffeine. On the downside, although it is an excellent description of how panic attacks escalate it does not explain why some people go on to develop panic disorder whereas others do not. Also, although most of the supporting research shows that panic sufferers do indeed show all of the cognitive biases suggested in Clark's model, it isn't entirely clear whether these biases develop and cause panic (and indeed how these biases develop) or whether having panic disorder creates these biases and they maintain the disorder. There is virtually no research that has looked at whether these cognitive biases are driven by biological mechanisms or are learnt through experience.

Learn to panic

Learning theorists have tried to explain panic disorder in terms of **'fear-of-fear'** (Goldstein & Chambless, 1978). This explanation hinges on low-level somatic sensations of anxiety or arousal (such as a heart murmur) which become associated with sudden bursts of anxiety of panic that generalise to other stimuli. So the low level symptoms act as conditioned stimuli (CS) that are associated with high levels of anxiety (the unconditioned stimuli) – see Chapter 2. However, McNally (1990) amongst others has criticised this explanation. First, the conditioned and unconditioned stimulus are both anxiety, so anxiety seems to indiscriminately act as a predictor and an outcome. This account also predicts that any occurrence of the CS should lead to a panic attack, yet this is not the case. A related point is that if the CSs occur without the presence of a panic attack then we'd predict that anxiety should extinguish over time – but it doesn't. Despite these problems, Bouton, Minkea and Barlow (2001) have argued that modern conditioning theory can in fact account for these anomalies.

Quick test

1. What is the connection between the fight-or-flight mechanism and panic disorder?

2. Can panic be conditioned?

3. What is Clark's cognitive model of panic?

Section 3

Can we explain social phobia?

Most of us experience some degree of anxiety in certain social situations (for example, when we're about to give a talk) yet for some this anxiety extends to situations that for most of us are not threatening (for example, going to a party). Most of the work on explaining social phobia has been done in the last ten to 20 years and so it is a developing topic of clinical and experimental research. This section looks at Clark and Well's (1995) cognitive model, which is fast emerging as the dominant theory of social anxiety. By the end of the section you should have some idea of the psychological processes behind this disorder.

The cognitive model

The cognitive theory of social phobia proposed by Clark and Wells (1995) has three stages.

1. Before a social interaction

On the basis of early experiences social phobics develop a set of assumptions about themselves and social situations that affect the way in which they interpret situations. For example, Hackmann, Clark & McManus (2000) found that patients with social phobia frequently report experiencing negative, distorted images when in anxiety-evoking situations and that these images are commonly linked to memories of adverse social events at the time of onset (an example being a boy who remembered being told that his hands were very sweaty). These assumptions lead social phobics to interpret normal social interactions in a very negative way. For example in one of my lectures I might interpret the fact that some students are yawning and gazing around staring into space as meaning that I'm being very boring (as opposed to a more positive interpretation such as 'all of my students have hangovers this morning'). These assumptions and the perceived social threat resulting from them trigger an anxiety programme, which is characterised by three interlinking components:

- somatic and cognitive symptoms
- safety behaviours and
- how the person processes themselves as a social object – see Figure 3.

Social phobics also tend to engage in detailed reviews of the possible outcomes of social interactions prior to entering them (we could call this a **pre-mortem**). Recollections of past failures, negative images of themselves, and predictions of poor performance and rejection dominate these thoughts. This pre-mortem can lead to complete avoidance of the situation, or simply put the person in a 'negative processing' state in which failure is expected and signs of acceptance are rejected.

2. During a social interaction

Figure 3 shows Clark & Wells' (1995) model of social phobia, which involves similar core processes to Clark's model of panic:

- **Somatic and cognitive symptoms:** these are reflexive responses triggered by the perception of threat (e.g. blushing, trembling, increased heart rate, mental blanks, lack of concentration, palpitations). Any one of these behaviours can be taken as further evidence of threat. This in turn can lead to further anxiety in much the same way that the vicious circle in panic is established (for example, trembling indicating loss of control leads to further anxiety which leads to more trembling).

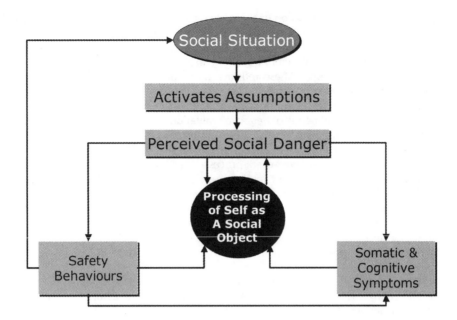

Figure 3: Clark and Wells' (1995) model of social phobia

- **Safety behaviours:** like panic patients, socially anxious individuals engage in safety behaviours to reduce social threat and prevent feared outcomes. These behaviours are often directly related to the outcomes they fear (for example avoiding eye contact, grasping a cup or glass tightly to avoid their hand shaking, or avoiding speaking for fear of being evaluated negatively because of saying something stupid). These behaviours often have detrimental effects: for example, reducing eye contact and avoiding talking can be perceived as disinterest with the conversation, and clutching a glass tightly actually increases trembling. As such, safety behaviours can prevent disconfirmation of false beliefs and can even increase the likelihood of the negative outcome.

- **Processing of the self as a social object:** the crucial component of this model is that social phobics show a shift in attention. When they believe they are under social scrutiny they focus inwardly and monitor their behaviours. This interoceptive information is used to construct an impression of what they believe others think of them. They form mental images of themselves as if from an external perspective (called the observer perspective), as if they were someone else looking at them. For example, a social phobic might assume that others notice that they are trembling and consequently think badly of them and they form a mental image of themselves trembling that is viewed from an external perspective. As such, they end up in a closed-feedback loop in which internally generated information heightens the belief in danger of negative evaluation and disconfirming information is ignored or avoided.

3. After a social interaction (post-event processing)

After a social interaction anxiety does not necessarily subside. Social phobics tend to conduct a **post-mortem** of the social event that typically involves thinking about ambiguous signs of social-acceptance (of which there will be many). The preoccupation will be with anxious feelings and negative self-perceptions and the ambiguous information will be reinterpreted as negative.

How the model works

This model is slowly beginning to gain empirical support. For example, when entering a social situation socially anxious individuals do seem to shift their attentional focus towards detailed monitoring and observation of themselves as a social object – neglecting external information (see Hofmann, 2000; Woody & Rodriguez, 2000; Wells & Papageorgiou, 1998). This tends to make them aware of the somatic and cognitive symptoms triggered by the perception of threat (e.g. blushing, trembling, increased heart rate, mental blanks, lack of concentration, palpitations). These reflexive behaviours are usually taken as further evidence of threat and create further anxiety (see Wells & Papageorgiou, 2001; Roth, Antony & Swinson, 2001). Furthermore, social phobics use in-situation safety behaviours as coping strategies to reduce the risk of negative evaluation by others (see Wells et al., 1995). The role of post-event processing has also been supported in that Rachman, Gruter-Andrew and Shafran (2000) constructed a post-event processing questionnaire and found a significant association between post-event processing and social anxiety. They emphasised that recollections of the social event tend to be recurrent and individuals with elevated levels of social anxiety spend long periods of time thinking about unsatisfactory social events in the past. Additionally, these thoughts have an intrusive quality that interferes with an individual's ability to concentrate. Despite efforts to resist thinking about past events, socially anxious people have reported a difficulty in attempts to forget or suppress information (Fehm & Margraf, 2002).

Finally, Clark & Wells (1995) suggest that the post-mortem produces increased levels of shame and many social phobics report a great deal of shame associated with social interactions. However, this idea is, as yet, untested.

It's easy to see many similarities between the cognitive models of panic and social phobia: both involve safety behaviours and bodily sensations and a cognitive bias in how threat is perceived. This is interesting given that panic and social phobia are treated as different disorders. Perhaps these similarities tell us that underlying the disorders are some common processes, but if this is the case is there a value in distinguishing the disorders? Also, like the cognitive model of panic, this explanation does a good job of describing what happens to a social phobic when they're placed in a social situation, but it does little to tell us why this happens. How do social anxiety and panic develop? Why do some of us get it and some do not? These are the questions that clinical researchers should hope to address in the near future.

Quick test

1. How do cognitions contribute to a social phobic's anxiety during a social situation?

2. What is post-event processing?

Section 4

Can we treat panic disorder and social phobia?

We've had a look at various theories of how panic attacks and social anxiety are maintained. The final part of this chapter examines how aspects of these models can be applied in therapeutic settings to help sufferers overcome their problem. We'll also look at the extent to which these therapies are effective.

─────── CRUCIAL CONCEPTS ───────

Behavioural experiments are tasks that allow patients to disconfirm their beliefs about certain situations, events or bodily sensations. For example, you might get a panic sufferer to deliberately hyperventilate to demonstrate that they won't have a heart attack.

Cognitive restructuring is done to change the biased beliefs that anxiety patients have through gathering information (this could be by using past events that are inconsistent with the patient's beliefs, or by using education such a medical article that highlights the real symptoms of a heart attack).

Treatment of panic

Drug therapy

Panic responds fairly well to tricyclic antidepressants such as imipramine, probably because these work on the neurotransmitter norepinephrine in the limbic system (see earlier). According to Lydiard, Brawman-Mintzer & Ballenger (1996) 60–90% of panic disorder patients have a reduction in panic attacks following these drugs and they also reduce agoraphobia. Although this finding lends support to a biological explanation, 20–50% of sufferers relapse once off the drug. These drugs also have unpleasant side effects such as blurred vision, dry mouth and urinal problems. Benzodiazepines (such as alprazolam or Xanax) suppress the central nervous system and affect functioning in the norepinephrine and serotonin neurotransmitter systems. It's not surprising, therefore, that they reduce panic attacks in 60–80% of patients (Ballenger, Burrows, Dupont & Lesser, *et al.* 1988). However, these drugs are addictive, people build a tolerance and so need increasing doses to have an effect, and withdrawal symptoms include irritability, anxiety, insomnia, seizures and paranoia. These drugs also have a 90% relapse rate and interfere with cognitive functioning (hinder driving, work etc.) so it seems that they just suppress the symptoms without really solving the problem.

Cognitive behaviour therapy (CBT)

CBT works by attempting to address the cognitive components of Clark's model. Despite what patients think, panic attacks are usually triggered by something: be it a subtle bodily cue (change in heart rate), an innocuous external event such as the world moving because of rapid circadic eye movements, or palpitations from coffee. Diaries and structured interviews can help the therapist to isolate these events and build up a personalised idea of what triggers the vicious circle.

Cognitive restructuring usually takes one of three forms.

- The first is to look at past events that are inconsistent with the patient's cognitions. For example, if I were having a panic attack in a lecture and some external event (such as a student coughing in the lecture) might distract me enough to stop the panic cycle. The therapist could then question my assumption that I was going to have a heart attack or faint by asking me 'Is coughing a good cure for heart disease?' Presumably I would agree not.

- Second, education is a useful tool in helping challenge assumptions about panic attacks. For example, Clark (1997) points out that panic patients who experience left-side pain can benefit from medical evidence that this type of pain is less predictive of heart attacks than right-side pain (although presumably it doesn't help those with right-side pain!).

- Finally, intrusive thoughts can be challenged by making these thoughts less severe. Clark (1997) uses the example of someone who frequently imagines themselves dead when having a panic attack. This image can be made less traumatic by training that person to bring themselves back to life in their mind.

Behavioural experiments can also be used to help patients to disconfirm their beliefs. One method is to induce the feared sensations (perhaps by encouraging self-focus, reading and dwelling on panic-related words, or hyperventilation) and then observing that the feared outcome (fainting, death, heart attack), does not happen. An alternative technique is to encourage patients to drop their safety behaviours (for example encourage exercise so the patient learns about all of the weird and wonderful things that your heart does during exercise, or not grabbing a stable object when dizzy to disconfirm the idea that the patient will fall over). These experiments allow patients to disconfirm their worst fears.

Treatment of social phobia

Drug therapy
Like panic, tricyclic antidepressants and benzodiazepines (Valium) can reduce anxiety in the short-term but are basically fairly useless as a long term solution because (1) they both have side-effects; and (2) relapse rates when the drugs are stopped are very high.

Cognitive behaviour therapy (CBT)
Therapy using CBT concentrates on several core areas of Clark and Wells' cognitive model:

Identify safety behaviours/somatic symptoms. The first step is to identify the components of the cognitive model that are specific to the individual. Most important is to identify safety behaviours that are used to try to prevent anxiety, and the somatic and cognitive symptoms. For example, patients often distort physical signs of stress (e.g. mild sweating can be transformed into a visual image of cascading waterfalls of sweat running down the person's head). Again, diaries and structured interviews are useful in isolating these events and 'personalising' the model.

Behavioural experiments can be set up using confederates in which a role-play of a feared situation is played out once using safety behaviours (e.g. avoiding eye contact, not speaking, rehearsing speech) and once without these behaviours (e.g. eye contact is enforced, and patients are encouraged to focus more on others than themselves). Patients rate their anxiety, how they felt and how they believe they appeared. Much to the patient's surprise their ratings may well be lower when safety behaviours are forbidden. Clark (1997) uses the example of someone who clutches a glass tightly to avoid their hand trembling who discovers through a behavioural experiment that they shake more when they clutch a glass tightly than when that safety behaviour is forbidden. Video and audio recordings of these staged interactions can be useful in disconfirming perceptions and to modify the biased observer-perspective images that social phobics tend to generate. If patients rate how they think they looked and performed, then watch a video and rate how they looked and performed, their ratings of the video are usually less than their predictions (for example, their image of their forehead as a Niagara falls of sweat is not confirmed by the video). Patients can also use these recordings for homework.

Given that patients hold distorted predictions about how others will evaluate them in social situations, it is important to test these predictions. One approach is to get the patient to deliberately perform a behaviour that they believe will make others reject them (such as spill a drink in public, say something stupid, or stammer) and then assess the degree to which others then evaluate them (in terms of what the patient believes is indicative of disapproval). In some situations the therapist may find it useful to take the lead (next time you see someone trip and throw a glass of wine across the room, don't worry, it's probably just a therapist disconfirming someone's beliefs about negative evaluation – so don't laugh at them!). Obviously the therapist must be careful to get the patient to carry out behaviours that will disconfirm their beliefs – it would be disastrous to reinforce it! Therapists sometimes use brief surveys on small samples; for example if the patient believes others will think her an alcoholic if her hand shakes, the therapist might carry out a short questionnaire asking people what symptoms they equate with alcoholism – a trembling hand won't be one of them!

Patients need to be made aware of the negative role of the post-mortem and should be encouraged to not dwell on social interactions. One technique is to get them to shout 'stop' whenever they begin to dwell on a social situation – this should distract their train of thought sufficiently for them to stop ruminating.

Finally, socially anxious people do hold deep-rooted negative assumptions and these need to be modified using Socratic questioning. For example, a social phobic who believes that someone hates them because that person wasn't talkative could be asked 'what other reasons might there be for that person not being talkative?' The social phobic after some thought might answer that perhaps the other person was tired, had a bad day at work, or was distracted.

How successful is therapy?

Panic
Clark *et al.* (1994) compared CBT with relaxation and Imipramine. They found that at three months cognitive therapy was better than the other two; at six months there was no difference between drugs and cognitive therapy but both were better than relaxation; however, after six months (and up to 15) 40% of drug patients relapsed compared to 5% of CBT. Across five studies cognitive therapy has around an 80% success rate (see Clark & Fairburn, 1997).

Social phobia
The efficacy of therapy for social phobia is nowhere near as clear-cut as panic, mainly because different techniques have been developed (e.g. anxiety management training (AMT), cognitive behavioural group treatment (CBGT) and exposure and cognitive restructuring (E+CT)) and most of the evidence is relatively recent. Mattick and Peters (1988) report only 38% success for their exposure and cognitive restructuring, and Heimberg *et al.* (1990) report 65% success in their group cognitive behaviour therapy. Clark & Wells, however, report that the types of techniques described in this chapter improve the fear of negative evaluation by about twice as much as other variations on this kind of therapy. Hofmann (2000) also recently reports that exposure and cognitive restructuring (using videos and didactic training) significantly reduced negative self-focused thoughts and improvement correlated with scores on well-used social anxiety questionnaire. So the jury is out on this form of therapy until more evidence is accumulated. Certainly is has some benefits but the long-term gains are, as yet, unknown.

Quick test

1. How are cognitive restructuring and behavioural experiments used in the treatment of panic and social phobia?
2. Can drugs be an effective treatment for panic and social phobia?
3. How successful is cognitive behaviour therapy for panic and social phobia?

Section 5

End of chapter assessment

Questions

1. What is panic disorder and how can it be treated?
2. What is social phobia and how is it treated?
3. Should panic and social phobia be thought of as different disorders?
4. Is panic disorder caused by an overactive fight-or-flight mechanism?
5. Compare the cognitive models of panic and social phobia.
6. What are the similarities (and differences) in the treatment of panic and social phobia?

Section 6

Further reading

Clark, D. M. (1989). Anxiety states: panic and generalized anxiety. In K. Hawton, P. M. Salkovskis, J. Kirk, and D. M. Clark (Eds.), *Cognitive Behaviour Therapy for Psychiatric Problems: A Practical Guide* (pp. 52–96). Oxford: Oxford University Press.

Clark, D. M. (1997). Panic disorder and social phobia. In D. M. Clark and C. G. Fairburn (Eds.), *Science and Practice of Cognitive Behaviour Therapy* (pp. 121–153). Oxford: Oxford University Press.

Clark, D. M. & Wells, A. (1995) A cognitive model of social phobia. In R. Heimberg, M. Liebowitz, D. A. Hope & F. R. Schneier (Eds.) *Social Phobia: Diagnosis, Assessment and Treatment*. New York: Guilford Press.

Chapter 5
Generalised anxiety disorder (GAD)

Chapter summary

This chapter explores a disorder characterised by an excessive worry about a variety of concerns: **generalised anxiety disorder** (**GAD**). We begin by looking at the key diagnostic features of GAD, and it turns out that worry is one of them. The next section, therefore, explores the differences between the worry that we all experience, and the worry experienced by people suffering from GAD. We'll see that people with GAD tend to worry for longer, and worry in a more catastrophic way. Before looking at other factors, we look at some contemporary theories that have tried to explain the nature of worry in GAD. We then move on to have a brief look at some of the cognitive biases found in people with GAD, and briefly overview the biological contribution to this disorder. The chapter ends by looking at how therapy attempts to address the worry found in GAD, and how behavioural and biological interventions can be used too.

Assessment targets

After reading this chapter you should be able to:

Target 1: **Explain the key diagnostic criteria for GAD. Question 1 at the end of this chapter tests you on this.**

Target 2: **Explain what pathological worry is. Question 2 at the end of this chapter tests you on this.**

Target 3: **Explain the different cognitive biases in GAD. Question 3 at the end of this chapter tests you on this.**

Target 4: **Explain the biological basis of GAD. Question 4 at the end of this chapter tests you on this.**

Target 5: **Explain how GAD is treated and relate the therapy back to the theories on which it is based. Question 5 at the end of this chapter tests you on this.**

Section 1

What is GAD?

Generalised anxiety disorder (or GAD as it is known) was not recognised as a psychological disorder until 1980 (in *DSM-III* – see Chapter 1). *DSM-IV* (APA, 1995) reports that the lifetime prevalence rate for GAD is about 5% (this is a reasonable average actually because other estimates tend to vary between about 2% and 7% across studies), and that 12% of patients in anxiety clinics have GAD. *DSM-IV* also reports that 55–60% of cases are female, which is getting close to a female to male ratio of 2:1. This section will look at the key diagnostic criteria for GAD and explore some of the problems with these criteria. As you read this section think about the similarities between this disorder and the other anxiety disorders about which you've already read in Chapters 3 and 4.

Diagnosis of GAD

It's quite easy to relate to GAD because its key feature is worry; people with GAD worry about stuff. However, they don't worry in quite the same way as most of us, they don't always worry about real concerns such as 'will I get my essay done on time?'; instead they feel anxious about literally everything. They will worry unnecessarily about how they're doing at work (even though all evidence may suggest they're doing very well) and about relationships, all of which seem perfectly natural. However, they'll worry over more trivial things as well, such as whether they might slightly overcook the potatoes for a dinner party, or worry about whether they should have toast for breakfast rather than cereal. Their worries literally cover everything and tend to flit from one topic to another, unlike the rest of us who tend to just focus on one specific major concern at a time. These feelings of worry are associated with high levels of distress and with concentration problems, sleep disruption, restlessness and high levels of muscle tension. Let's now have a look at the key diagnostic features from *DSM–IV*.

CRUCIAL DIAGNOSIS

The *Diagnostic and Statistical Manual of Mental Disorders* (*DSM-IV*) characterises GAD as follows (taken from pages 435–6):

A. Excessive anxiety and worry (apprehensive expectation), occurring more days than not for at least six months, about a number of events or activities (such as work or school performance).

B. The person finds it difficult to control the worry.

C. The anxiety and worry are associated with three (or more) of the following six symptoms (with at least some symptoms present for more days than not for the past six months). Note: only one item is required in children:

- restlessness or feeling keyed up or on edge;
- being easily fatigued;
- difficulty concentrating or mind going blank;
- irritability;
- muscle tension;
- sleep disturbance (difficulty falling or staying asleep, or restless, unsatisfying sleep).

D. Not better explained by another Axis I disorder.

E. The anxiety, worry, or physical symptoms cause clinically significant distress or impairment in social, occupational, or other important areas of functioning.

F. The disturbance is not due to the direct physiological effects of a substance (e.g. a drug of abuse, a medication) or a general medical condition (e.g. hyperthyroidism) and does not occur exclusively during a mood disorder, a psychotic disorder, or a pervasive developmental disorder.

The key parts of these diagnostic criteria are that the worry must be uncontrollable, happen most days and persist for more than six months. The worry should also be associated with various physical symptoms (restlessness, sleep disturbance, etc.). As with most disorders, it is important to rule out a better diagnosis. This is particularly important in GAD because of potential overlap with the other anxiety disorders. Therefore the focus of the anxiety and worry should not be confined to features of another Axis I disorder: the anxiety or worry should not be about having a panic attack (as in panic disorder – chapter 4), being embarrassed in public (as in social phobia – Chapter 4), intrusive thoughts (as in obsessive-compulsive disorder – Chapter 6), being away from home or close relatives (as in separation anxiety disorder), gaining weight (as in anorexia nervosa – see Chapter 7), having multiple physical complaints (as in somatisation disorder), or having a serious illness (as in hypochondriasis). Finally, as with all disorders, physical causes should be ruled out and the worry must significantly impair the person's functioning.

─────── CRUCIAL CASE STUDY ───────

Tim had always been a 'worrier', although over the last few months he felt this had got 'out of control'. He remembered his mother telling him he had been difficult as a baby, being easily upset and taking a long time to settle at night. He worried about 'everything': the chance of physical danger occurring or people thinking badly of him for some reason. He thought he probably didn't worry about particularly different things from other people, he just thought he worried about them 'all the time'. He did, however, feel that he noticed danger everywhere, although never felt confident that he would be able to do anything that would be any help. His last relationship had broken up, because his partner felt he was constantly asking for reassurance. Tim was frequently kept awake at night with thoughts going around his head, and although he generally thought they were unimportant he was unable to dismiss them.

GAD criteria

The good aspects of the diagnostic criteria are that they are very aware of overlap with other anxiety disorders and that they appreciate that worry is a fairly everyday activity for a good many people. As such, great care has been taken to distinguish between everyday levels of worry, and the levels at which it becomes a disorder by distinguishing both the severity (in terms of the physical symptoms it causes) and duration (it has to be persistent for over six months) of the worry. The potentially problematic aspects of these criteria are that there are still some vague quantifiers. For example, what constitutes a significant impairment to functioning: failure to turn up to work, or just feeling like you're not working as effectively as you used to? Second, there are still some fairly arbitrary limits: why does it have to persist for six months rather than five or seven? Why do you have to have three of the six physical symptoms? If you have only two does that mean you don't have GAD? Of course, these vague quantifiers and arbitrary cut-offs are unavoidable, and it's left to the discretion of a trained clinician to adapt these criteria as they see fit in a particular case.

Quick test

1. What are the key diagnostic features of GAD?
2. What are the good and bad aspects of the diagnostic criteria?

Section 2

What is worry and why does it persist?

Worry is a word that we all intuitively understand and we probably all know what it is like to worry. Nevertheless, it is important for researchers and clinicians to define the term so that it can be distinguished. Also, if worry is an everyday activity for most people, then we need to know how the process differs in people with GAD: is there a qualitative difference in the way that GAD sufferers worry? This section looks first at how worry is defined and then looks at ways in which worry is different in GAD to normal experience.

Defining worry

Worry appears to have many similarities with other thought processes in the anxiety disorders. For example, descriptions of obsessions (see Chapter 6), worry and ruminations (see Chapters 2, 3 and 8) are often difficult to disentangle: the terms often seem interchangeable (Davey, Field & Startup, in press). However, the processes can be distinguished. For example, Turner, Beidel & Stanley (1992) distinguished obsessions and worry in three respects:

- worries typically focus on daily concerns;
- obsessions may be more intrusive than worries;
- and obsessions lead to compulsions.

Worry and rumination are particularly hard to disentangle: both are repetitive, iterative and somewhat uncontrollable thought processes that are associated with anxiety (Davey & Tallis, 1994), and depression (Borkovec, 1994). However, worries and ruminations differ in terms of their frequency, duration, the ratio of verbal to visual image content, how much they interfere with other thoughts, their egodystonic nature (whether they are at odds with how the person perceives themselves), and the emotions they elicit (Langlois, Freeston & Ladouceur, 2000): worry is typically expressed verbally, is more distracting, more realistic, more voluntary and is associated with a stronger urge to act (Wells & Morrison, 1994) whereas ruminations are typically egodystonic, can occur through images and impulses as well as verbal thought, and are more intrusive (Turner, *et al.* 1992). Worry also appears to focus on future events (Borkovec, 1994; MacLeod, 1994) whereas rumination typically focuses on past events and experiences (Martin & Tesser, 1989).

CRUCIAL CONCEPT

Perseveration is engaging in some kind of cognitive or behavioural activity way beyond its utility. It's persevering with a thought process or a behaviour even though it no longer serves a useful function.

Differences between normal and pathological worry

In many ways there are very few differences between normal and pathological worry. Craske, Rapee, Jackel, and Barlow, (1989) classified the worries of 19 GAD patients and 26 non-anxious controls and found that they fell into five categories:

- family, home and interpersonal relationships;
- finances;
- work or school;
- illness, injury and health; and
- miscellaneous.

Although there were no reliable differences in the content of these worries or the anxiety they produced, GAD patients reported a significantly greater proportion of worries about illness, health and injury than controls, but the controls experienced more worries about finances. However, one factor that did significantly distinguish the groups was the controllability of the worries. This is a finding that has been replicated in other contexts (e.g. Wells & Morrison, 1994, Rapee, 1991; Kent & Jambunathan, 1989).

There are two reasons why worry might become uncontrollable. The first is that pathological worriers might use worry as a means to avoid other forms of thought that are associated with negative feelings (Borkovec & Inz 1990). GAD patients may use worry as a form of cognitive avoidance, and therefore it becomes self-rewarding: the person worries, this worry averts a negative feeling (it may also prevent full access to fear information in memory), and so the person worries more (because worry is rewarded). Think back to Mowrer's theory in Chapter 3 – the idea is similar. The second possibility is that patients with GAD try too hard to control their worrying. When people try not to think about things, known as **thought suppression** (see Purdon, 1999), it makes them think about it more and this is called a **rebound effect** (more on this in Chapter 6). So worry may become uncontrollable in people with GAD because they're trying so hard to stop worrying that they get a rebound effect – they worry more!

CRUCIAL CONCEPT

Catastrophising is, in the worry literature, seen as the tendency to iterate negative outcomes of a potential worry. It usually takes the form of a 'what if?' type questioning style and usually leads the worrier to perceive progressively worse and worse outcomes to the worry topic (see Davey *et al.*, in press). So for example, if you were worried about failing your exam you might think 'What if I fail this exam?, Well, I won't pass my degree. If I don't pass my degree then I won't get a job. If I don't get a job then I'll have no money. If I don't have money I'll have to go begging. If I go begging I'll end up a drug addict. If I end up a drug addict I'll probably die of a heroin overdose in a gutter. If I die of drugs I'll go to hell. If I go to hell, Satan will feast daily on my entrails...' and so on. So it's taking a worry and seeing progressively worse implications from it.

CRUCIAL STUDY

Davey and Levy (1998) looked at the way in which 'worriers' and 'non-worriers' catastrophise. Across six ingenious studies, these groups were asked to catastrophise not just about personal worries but also about something they couldn't possibly have ever worried about before: being the Statue of Liberty! Sometimes they were asked to worry positively about situations (what's good about being the Statue of Liberty) and sometimes negatively (what worries you about being the Statue of Liberty?). They found that worriers were willing to catastrophise both a positive aspect of their life and worry about a new hypothetical worry (being the Statue of Liberty) significantly more than non-worriers. So worriers seemed to display a general iterative style that was independent of whether the task was positive or negative. Interestingly, worriers also tended to couch their worries in terms of personal inadequacies, and personal inadequacy became a feature of their catastrophising regardless of the worry topic.

Another difference in pathological worry, therefore, is a tendency to worry catastrophically, that is, worriers tend to catastrophise when they worry. Interestingly other evidence (see Davey *et al.*, in press) seems to suggest that forms of iterative thinking such as rumination can actually increase anxiety and catastrophising. The implication is that worriers (and GAD patients) persist in worrying for longer than 'non-worriers' and this leads them to contemplate catastrophic consequences. So what makes them persist?

One factor in perseveration is negative mood, which has been shown to lead to more extensive processing (Schwarz & Bless, 1991). In fact, Startup and Davey (2001; see also Davey *et al.*, in press) have tried to explain worrying in terms of a 'mood-as-input' hypothesis. This hypothesis states that perseveration on a task is a function of both the mood of the person when they begin the task, and the internal rule that they have about when to stop the task. The idea is that there are basically two rules that people use to decide when to stop a task: these can be summarised as 'stop when I feel like stopping', or 'stop when I have solved the problem'. Startup and Davey suggest that when working on a task, worriers ask themselves (explicitly or implicitly) 'have I solved the problem?' rather than asking themselves 'do I feel like stopping?'. Given that worriers adopt this 'have I solved the problem' rule for stopping, then if they are in a positive mood they interpret their positive mood as a sign that they have attained or made progress towards solving the problem. However, if they happen to be in a negative mood, they interpret this mood as a sign that they have not made progress towards solving the problem and so they continue. This interaction of stop rules and mood can explain why worriers persist in worrying.

CRUCIAL CONCEPT

Meta-worry is the negative appraisal of one's own worrying. In short it's worrying about the fact you're worrying!

A final difference is what Wells (1995) has called 'meta-worry'. Meta-worry is characterised by themes such as 'worrying will make me crazy', 'other people don't worry like I do', 'worrying thoughts will cause bad things to happen' and 'my worrying is out of control.'

Wells claims it is this meta-worry that distinguishes GAD patients from everyone else, and that this explains Craske *et al*.'s (1989) finding that the content of GAD patients' worries does not differ from those of 'normal' people. Wells argues that negative attitudes about worrying are likely to develop from, amongst other places, the media, family and other social and cultural domains. Once negative attributes to worrying develop they may be exacerbated by comparing your own worrying behaviour to that of others, or by the fact that any increased propensity to worry will lead to a greater probability that your worrying will, by chance, become associated with something negative. This all builds up to increase the amount a person worries about the fact that they worry. This theory has many similarities with cognitive models of obsessive-compulsive disorder (see Chapter 6), which characterises this disorder in terms of unwanted thoughts, concerns that those thoughts will result in harm and subsequent concern about these thoughts leading to attempts to control these thoughts. This highlights an important point that there may be core processes underlying all of the anxiety disorders.

Quick test

1. What are the differences between 'normal' and pathological worry?

2. How does mood contribute to perseverative and catastrophic worry?

3. What is meta-worry?

Section 3

Do we think ourselves into being anxious?

The previous section concentrated on one particular aspect of GAD: worry. Although the way in which people worry when they have GAD could be seen as a cognitive bias in itself, this section deals explicitly with other cognitive biases found in GAD patients. We'll look first at attentional biases and then misinterpretation of ambiguous information.

Attentional biases

Using the emotional stroop task (see Chapter 2) it has been shown that anxious individuals, and specifically, individuals with GAD, are slower to name the colours of words when those words are threatening, even when those words are presented too quickly to consciously perceive them (Mathews & MacLeod, 1994; Mogg, Bradley, Williams & Mathews, 1993). This suggests that people who have GAD, or who are high in natural levels of anxiety, are vigilant for threatening stimuli.

Misinterpretation of ambiguous information

In a classic study Eysenck, Mogg, May, Richards and Mathews (1991) showed anxious, recovered anxious, and non-anxious individuals 32 ambiguous sentences. Two examples are: 'The two men watched as the chest was opened' and 'The doctor examined little Emma's growth'. Later on, the same individuals were presented with both a positive and negative interpretation of each sentence and they had to identify which sentence they had read earlier on. For example, they were shown a negative sentence such as 'The doctor looked at little Emma's cancer' and a positive one such as 'The doctor measured little Emma's height.' Of course the participants had seen neither sentence but Eysenck *et al*. counted the number of negative interpretations that each person chose. Anxious individuals chose many more negative statements than non-anxious individuals.

Implications of cognitive biases

The cognitive biases described above imply that people suffering from anxiety perceive more threat in their environment than people without anxiety disorders. The suggestion is, therefore, that these people live in a relatively more anxiety-inducing world than people without these biases. Put another way, they detect more threats in their environment than people without the disorder and, therefore, it isn't surprising that they are more anxious: they see threats that others don't.

Quick test

What cognitive biases do people suffering from GAD have?

Section 4

Are we born anxious?

If people with GAD have a general sensitivity to threatening material, then perhaps this develops as a result of biological factors. As with all of the disorders in this book, biological explanations hinge on neurotransmitters. Although biological models of GAD are in their infancy, in this section we'll look at whether genetic factors have a role to play, and which neurotransmitters are implicated in GAD.

Genetic factors

Studies looking at genetic factors have remained inconsistent. One major twin study does seem to suggest a genetic predisposition for GAD (Kendler, Neale, Kessler, & Heath, 1992); however it appears that the genes that have been isolated predict a general neurotic vulnerability rather than specifically predicting GAD.

GABA

The only biological theory of GAD came from the discovery in the 1950s that the family of drugs known as benzodiazepines reduce anxiety. Benzodiazepines increase the activity of a neurotransmitter known as gamma-aminobutyric acid (or GABA to its friends). This neurotransmitter carries inhibitory messages between neurons so when it binds to a neuronal receptor that neuron is inhibited from firing. This has led to the idea that people with GAD may have a deficiency of GABA in their brains (and hence are anxious). As with most psychological disorders, the area in which this neurotransmitter acts is the limbic system, which we have seen controls emotional, physiological and behavioural responses (see Chapter 2). However, this theory is very much in its infancy and further studies (especially on humans) are needed to unearth the precise role of GABA in GAD.

Quick test

What biological factors have been implicated in GAD?

Section 5

How is GAD treated?

As you should have noticed by now, most of what is known about GAD hinges on cognitive biases and biology. Therefore it's no surprise to discover that cognitive therapies and drug therapies are what clinicians generally use to treat this disorder. This section looks at some of the cognitive techniques that are applied in therapy, and also discusses the efficacy of these treatments, and treatments based on drugs.

How cognitive therapy works

All of the therapies we've come across so far (Chapters 3 and 4) have combined both aspects of cognitive therapy and behavioural therapy. In all of these cases, exposure has been a central part of the therapeutic process. However exposure, in the traditional sense, has much less of a role to play in GAD because there are no specific triggers for the anxiety: the patient is constantly anxious about everything so to what on earth do you expose them? Initially this led therapies to focus on general relaxation, in the hope that patients would simply learn to be calm. However, a more recent technique that has been applied is to expose patients to their cognitions. This may sound a little odd, but essentially the idea is that they are forced to imagine the worst possible consequence of something about which they're worrying for a prolonged period (until they are relaxed) and then to consider other possible explanations. For example, if they are worried that they are not doing very well at work, then they imagine a horrible situation (e.g. the boss being angry with them) and then, when calm, they generate benign reasons why he might be angry (he's having a bad day). This, first and foremost, helps them to get used to their cognitions, but also helps them to practise not misinterpreting ambiguous information. So, it treats the anxious response and the cognitive distortion.

Worry has only been recently introduced into models of GAD and so early therapies focused primarily on basic cognitive techniques such as those used for depression (Chapter 8 will give you some more detail on these) rather than addressing worry. Although the use of these cognitive strategies (which change core dysfunctional beliefs, challenge misinterpretations and improve self-esteem) in conjunction with some behavioural techniques have proved to have some efficacy (see below), the state-of-the-art view is that techniques need to be added that specifically address worry. For example, Wells and Butler (1997) have argued that dysfunctional beliefs about worry have to be specifically addressed through behavioural experiments (see previous chapter) and cognitive techniques that target the negative beliefs that drive the meta-worry. So if someone is worried that they will lose control, they could be encouraged to try to lose control of their worrying; the patient should discover that even if they try, they cannot lose control. Likewise, if they believe that worrying will result in bad things happening, they can be encouraged to worry more or less to see that their level of worry doesn't change the number of bad things that happen. In fact many of the techniques described in the next chapter can be applied to GAD.

Drug therapy

Drug therapy simply hinges on giving patients Benzodiazepines to reduce their anxiety. Some examples are Xanax, Librium, Serax and most famously Valium. These drugs increase functional levels of GABA in the brain. These drugs have unfortunate side effects such as memory loss, depression, and damage to bodily organs and can be physically addictive. A newer drug acts not on GABA, but on serotonin receptors. This drug is from the azaspirones class and is called Buspirone (or BuSpar).

How successful is therapy?

Benzodiazepines are actually excellent in the short term for some people. However, the long-term gains are negligible, and even people who benefit from them short-term quickly relapse once off the drugs. Buspirone also seems to have an effect on GAD and, as far as we currently know, has far fewer side effects than benzodiazepines (Apter & Allen, 1999).

In terms of cognitive-based therapies, CBT has been found to be beneficial compared to only behavioural-based therapies, by Butler, Fennell, Robson & Gelder (1991). Butler and her colleagues found that CBT produced greater and more stable cognitive changes than behaviour therapy and these gains had increased at a six-month follow-up. A couple of years later Borkovec and Costello (1993) reported similar gains using cognitive techniques specifically aimed at GAD. They reported long-term gains compared to just relaxation and high end-of-therapy functioning in nearly 60% of patients. Durham *et al.* (1994) reported similar success compared to brief psychodynamic therapy and anxiety management strategies, and Warren and Zgourides (1991) suggest that cognitive-based therapies are more beneficial than drug therapies. Finally, therapy also seems to reduce selective interference effects (similar to those elicited by the emotional stroop task) in anxious patients (Mathews, Mogg, Kentish & Eysenck, 1995). As yet, there are no studies to indicate whether techniques to address meta-worry improve the benefits of cognitive therapy further.

Quick test

1. How is worry addressed in cognitive-based therapies for GAD?

2. Which drugs are effective for treating GAD?

Section 6

End of chapter assessment

Questions

1. What is GAD?

2. What is pathological worry? How does it differ from 'normal' worry?

3. How do the cognitive biases in GAD differ from those in other anxiety disorders (read the other chapters before trying to answer this)?

4. Can we explain GAD in purely biological terms?

5. Describe a cognitive–behavioural treatment for GAD. Why should it be effective?

Section 7

Further reading

Davey, G. C. L. & Tallis, F. (Eds.) (1994). *Worrying: Perspectives on Theory, Assessment and Treatment* (pp. 115–34). Chichester: Wiley. (This book is quite high level but really does tell you everything you need to know about worry.)

Wells, A. (1997). *Cognitive Therapy of Anxiety Disorders: A Practice Manual and Conceptual Guide.* Chichester: Wiley. (Chapter 8 is a very accessible source for theory and treatment of GAD.)

Chapter 6
Obsessive compulsive disorder (OCD)

Chapter summary

This chapter looks at the last of the anxiety disorders: **obsessive compulsive disorder** (**OCD**). First, we look at the difference between obsessions and compulsions by looking at the *DSM* criteria. We also see that some of these symptoms taken in isolation are not too different from everyday experience. We move on to look at explanations of OCD, first by seeing whether learning theory tells us anything about how OCD develops. We then turn to cognitive theories, which elaborate on the ways in which sufferers of OCD interpret their thoughts differently (for example they believe that their thoughts are indicative of future action and that they have responsibility for preventing future catastrophes). However, these theories don't explain from where these maladaptive processes come and so we look at the role of biology and the frontal cortex-caudate nucleus-thalamus pathway. The chapter ends by looking at how OCD is treated. We'll see that exposure and response prevention (ERP) combined with cognitive therapy can be an effective way to address this disturbing disorder.

Assessment targets

After reading this chapter you should be able to:

Target 1: Explain the key diagnostic criteria for obsessive compulsive disorder. Question 1 at the end of this chapter tests you on this.

Target 2: Explain the behavioural and biological explanations of OCD. Question 2 at the end of this chapter tests you on this.

Target 3: Explain the cognitive model of obsessive compulsive disorder and know its limitations. Question 3 at the end of this chapter tests you on this.

Target 4: Explain how obsessive compulsive disorder is treated, relate the therapy back to the theories on which it is based, and know how successful therapy is. Question 4 at the end of this chapter tests you on this.

Section 1

What is obsessive compulsive disorder?

Imagine what life would be like if every time you walked into a room you first had to touch the door handle 16 times; if you lost count, or didn't touch the handle in exactly the right kind of way, you'd have to start from the beginning until you were satisfied that you'd touched it 16 times in exactly the correct way. What about if you constantly had thoughts about sexually assaulting people that just 'popped' into your head even though this activity is completely abhorrent to you; but you're worried that these thoughts mean that one day you will assault someone? These are examples of the problems faced by people suffering from obsessive compulsive disorder (OCD). When most of us think of OCD, we probably conjure up the light-hearted image of someone who has to check that they've turned the gas off before leaving for a holiday, or who keeps looking in their bag to make sure their passport hasn't mysteriously vanished since the last time they looked. However, OCD is rarely so benign. This section will look at the prevalence of OCD and how clinical psychologists diagnose it by looking at the difference between obsessions and compulsions.

Diagnosis of OCD

OCD was originally believed to be quite rare, occurring in less than 0.1% of the population. However recent evidence suggests rates of 1–3% (Karno & Golding, 1991) – similar to the rates of other anxiety disorders (see Chapters 3–5). The onset of OCD is typically between 6 to 15 years of age in males but slightly higher in females who develop the disorder between the ages of 20 to 29. Males typically exhibit a high prevalence of checking behaviours whereas women more frequently report washing rituals.

Although OCD is classified as an anxiety disorder it is rather unusual in that primarily it is a thought disorder, not an anxiety disorder. However, it is classified as an anxiety disorder because the thoughts and associated compulsions cause sufferers considerable anxiety. However, it is possible that in the future OCD will be declassified as an anxiety disorder. OCD is an extremely debilitating and frustrating disorder that interferes with virtually every aspect of everyday life, is chronic if left untreated and usually leaves its sufferers utterly desperate.

OCD is characterised by the everyday intrusion into conscious thinking of intense, repetitive, personally abhorrent, absurd and alien thoughts (**obsessions**), leading to the endless repetition of specific acts or to the rehearsal of bizarre and irrational mental and behavioural rituals (**compulsions**). As such, clinical manifestations of OCD may be very diverse. Obsessions and compulsions are not the same, and before we look at theories of OCD we must understand the distinction between these two things.

CRUCIAL CONCEPTS

DSM–IV defines **obsessions** as 'Recurrent and persistent thoughts, impulses or images that are experienced at some time during the disturbance, as intrusive and inappropriate and that cause marked anxiety or distress.'
Compulsions on the other hand are defined by *DSM–IV* as 'repetitive behaviours or mental acts that the person feels driven to perform in response to an obsession, or according to rules that must be applied rigidly.'

CRUCIAL DIAGNOSIS

In addition, to meet *DSM* for obsessions (as defined above) the following must be true:

A. The obsessions (as defined above) must not simply be excessive worries about real life problems.
B. The person must attempt to ignore or suppress the obsessive thoughts, impulses or images, or neutralise them with some other thought or action.
C. Finally, the person must recognise that the obsessive thoughts, impulses or images are a product of their own mind (not imposed from without).

In terms of compulsions, *DSM-IV* insists that:

D. These compulsions (behaviours or mental acts) are carried out to prevent or reduce distress or avert some dreaded event or situation and are either excessive or not realistically connected with what they are designed to neutralise or prevent.

The *DSM-IV* criteria for OCD also have several important features that are similar to other anxiety disorders (think back to the diagnostic criteria in Chapters 3–5). Like specific phobias, the person has to recognise that their response (in this case the obsessions or compulsions) are excessive or unreasonable. Also, like specific phobias, social phobia, panic disorder and GAD, the symptoms (in this case the obsessions and compulsions) must cause marked distress or significantly interfere with the person's normal routine, functioning or relationships. Also, like other anxiety disorders, *DSM-IV* includes two usual qualifiers: the disorder must not be better described by a different classification, and the symptoms must not result from substance abuse or a medical condition.

Describing the disorder

We now have an insight into the formal definition of the disorder. However, this doesn't give us a true flavour of what a typical sufferer experiences. We'll now turn to look at some examples of obsessions and compulsions. We'll start with obsessions.

The term obsession is really slightly misleading: it conjures up images of someone plastering their bedroom with loads of posters of Kurt Cobain (or in my case Fugazi!), or whoever your idol might be, and buying all of their records. In fact, we've seen that obsessions are not like this at all: they are uncontrollable and intrusive thoughts—something that is completely involuntary and involves passive experience (not an active admiration of your hero). The passivity of experience is key: the sufferer has no control whatsoever over their thoughts and intrusions.

CRUCIAL STUDY

Probably the most detailed analysis of the types of symptoms experienced in OCD was conducted by Akthar and colleagues (1975). They found that the vast majority of intrusive thoughts involved doubts, thoughts, fears and impulses (of course these sets are not mutually exclusive), and intrusive images were less prevalent: doubts (74%), thinking (34%), fears (26%), impulses (17%), images (7%), and other (2%). They also discovered that there were recurring themes in different people's obsessions, and these themes were contamination, dirt, disease, illness (46%); violence and aggression (29%); moral and religious topics (11%); symmetry and sequence (27%); sex (10%); and other (22%).

As you might expect, obsessions can take many forms: as well as varying types (thoughts, impulses, images) the content can vary enormously from simply doubts (e.g. did I switch the light off?), to impulses (e.g. to throw myself under a train), to bizarre intrusions (e.g. the image of pulling the skin from your face). Some actual examples are (some of these are taken from Davison & Neale, 2000; Lemma, 1996):

- doubt: 'Did I lock the door?' (male, 28);
- thought that he had cancer (male, 46);
- thought and image that he had knocked someone down in his car (male, 29);
- impulse to have sex with his daughter (male, 49);
- impulse and thought to shout obscenities in church (female, 19; male 28);
- image of her corpse rotting away (female, 27);
- impulse to drink from an inkpot and to strangle their son (male, 41).

These examples highlight the themes described by Akhtar *et al.* (1975) and as you can see obsessions generally seem to fall into certain common groups that can all be broadly defined in terms of being socially unacceptable (either morally, spiritually or physically). For example contamination, illness, disease, dirt, and death all have social stigmas and many of the sexual practices that OCD sufferers have thoughts about are morally unacceptable in many cultures (e.g. sex with children). Violent and aggressive acts violate society's moral code, and religious themes tap into basic universal concepts of 'good' and 'bad' and 'right' and 'wrong'. Most of these themes also, perhaps coincidentally, link with disgust, which is one of six universal emotions (Ekman & Friesen, 1971), this is interesting when you consider that disgust has also been linked to other anxiety disorders (such as spider phobia, Davey 1994). Finally, the themes often have a contemporary flavour to them, reflecting current issues such as chemical contamination and highly publicised diseases (e.g. AIDS).

Compulsions differ from obsessions in that they are conscious, voluntary actions; they can be **overt** (behavioural) such as cleaning, checking, hoarding and orderliness, or **covert** (cognitive) such as imagining sequences, or repeating 'cancellation thoughts'. Typically these rituals have a rigid sequence of steps with a clearly defined beginning and end. Compulsions vary from being relatively logical (e.g. there is a logical connection between obsessional beliefs about contamination and the washing of hands) to extremely arbitrary (e.g. it is not clear why someone might feel the need to touch the ground after swallowing saliva). Some examples (taken from Davison & Neale, 2000; Rapoport, 1989) are as follows:

- scanning the pages of a book for the word 'life' after having read the word 'death';
- touching the ground after swallowing saliva;
- driving back to check he hadn't knocked someone down in his car;
- counting '6, 5, 8, 3, 7, 4' in his head;
- hand-washing.

These compulsions will often have very specific rules and will be repeated until they have been done 'properly'. For example, someone who taps a door 14 times before they enter a room may have a specific way in which these taps must be completed. Failure on a single tap requires the full ritual to be repeated. It is these compulsions that disrupt everyday activities. Try to imagine holding down a job if you had to wash your hands 200 times a day, could not read text if it contained the word 'death', or had to tap the floor 23 times in a particular way every time you entered a room.

CRUCIAL CASE STUDY

Obsessions and compulsions are intrinsically linked (see Figure 4). Once an intrusive thought has occurred, or an obsession has been triggered, this generally provokes anxiety and distress. An obsession usually has an associated compulsion that serves the function of reducing this distress in some way. For example, Rapoport (1989) reports a man in his 40s who had a death obsession. Whenever he read the word 'death' (or similar) he believed that he would in some way contaminate other objects (especially the future) if he looked at anything with his eyes. Having read the word death, he would not read on (for fear of contaminating the future) and would not look up from the book (for fear of contaminating people), but would read previous pages of the book to find a word to cancel out the contamination. These 'neutralising' words had specific rules (i.e. 'life' would cancel 'death', 'living' would cancel 'dying', but 'living' would not cancel 'death'). This checking ritual could take long periods of time because as he checked he would sometimes come across other death-related words that would then also have to be neutralised. So the connection between compulsions and obsessions is that the compulsions act in some way to neutralise the obsessive thought.

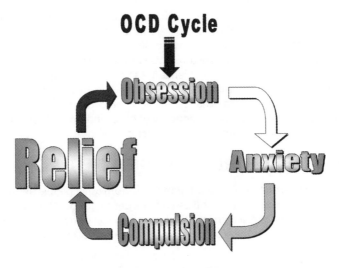

Figure 4: The OCD cycle

Quick test

1. What is an obsession?

2. What is a compulsion?

3. How are obsessions and compulsions linked?

Section 2

Explanations of OCD

In the previous section we learnt that OCD is characterised by disturbing intrusive thoughts and ritualistic compulsions. The next section looks at the explanations that have been put forward to explain how these obsessions and compulsions come about. As you read each of the explanations think about the extent to which they merely describe what goes on in OCD and the degree to which they actually provide a causal explanation of why some people develop this disorder and others don't.

Behavioural explanations of OCD

The behavioural explanation is based on Mowrer's (1960) two-factor theory of anxiety that we came across in Chapter 3. To refresh your memory, this theory argued that stimuli acquire aversive properties through classical conditioning (think back to little Albert) and this fear is maintained over time by avoidance because that behaviour is always associated with a positive outcome (a reduction in fear or, if you successfully avoid the stimulus altogether, no fear at all). Avoidance also ensures that you never disconfirm your belief that the fear-evoking stimulus is unpleasant. In OCD these ideas are applied in a similar way: obsessions are thought to become aversive through association with some traumatic event or situations. The rituals develop subsequently as a means to neutralise (or avoid) these obsessions and so ritualistic behaviour is reinforced.

There are plenty of problems with this account, not least of which is that most obsessions are fairly distressing in their own right (would you not find the thought of killing a child distressing in its own right without needing to have that thought occur in conjunction with some external aversive event?), so it's unlikely that these obsessions acquire aversive properties through conditioning. Also, the behavioural account cannot explain why these thoughts recur and doesn't explain cases in which obsessions occur but compulsions don't. In fact, Jones and Menzies (1998) showed very little retrospective evidence for learning pathways in OCD. What's more, Rachman and de Silva (1978) reported that 90% of the normal population experience intrusive thoughts with the same content and form as those in OCD sufferers. If 90% of people experience these sorts of thoughts then why do only 1–3% of people develop the disorder? Learning theory would predict a much higher incidence. This gives us a clue to what might lie behind the disorder: either there is a qualitative difference in the severity or frequency of obsessions in OCD, or people with OCD must interpret their obsessions differently to other people.

Cognitive explanations of OCD

If people with OCD interpret their thoughts differently from other people then we can look to cognitive approaches to discover what these differences might be. The last ten to 15 years have seen a vast amount of research into the basic cognitive differences in those with OCD compared to those without. There seem to be many cognitive abnormalities in those with OCD:

Responsibility

People with OCD have an inflated sense of responsibility over outcomes (Foa *et al.*, 2001). In general terms they seem to possess a cognitive distortion such that they perceive any influence over an outcome as meaning they have responsibility over that outcome. This distortion leads to the belief that if they omit to do something, they may end up harming themselves or others. You can find themes of responsibility in most of the examples we've come across in this chapter – 'I have run someone over', 'if I look at someone with eyes that have seen the word death I will contaminate them (or kill them)', 'impulse to strangle his son', 'if I blaspheme in church, I will burn in hell.' Interestingly, situations that would normally evoke checking produce little anxiety or few checking rituals when responsibility is shared with a therapist (Roper & Rachman, 1976). This perception of responsibility leads to attempts to neutralise or reduce responsibility through overt behaviours (driving back to see if you have run someone over) or through covert rituals. These rituals often stem from 'magical' thinking ('if I look at the word life I will neutralise the word death').

Thought = action

Another common misinterpretation in OCD is that thought equals action; for example, if you think about killing your child then you will kill your child. A similar phenomenon is the belief that thinking about killing your child is as bad as doing it. This is known as the **thought–action fusion** (see Rachman, 1997).

Going crazy

OCD sufferers generally interpret their intrusive thoughts as being indicative of them 'going crazy' (perhaps because they believe these thoughts to be indicative of actions, or because of the inflated sense of responsibility that they have).

Control

The inflated sense of responsibility and misinterpretations bring with them a need to control thoughts (so that no harm will come to others). OCD sufferers believe that they should have control over their thoughts. One way in which they try to do this is by trying to stop their intrusive thoughts (**thought suppression**—see Purdon, 1999). Sadly, when you try to suppress thoughts you get a rebound effect: the frequency of these thoughts increases. You can try this yourself, by telling yourself that you must not, under any circumstances, think about something (for example, the devil) for the next 60 seconds. Time yourself 60 seconds and watch as the devil pops into your head more times than you ever thought imaginable! These attempts at thought suppression are also accompanied by a preoccupation (an attentional bias) towards stimuli and thoughts relevant to the obsession (see Clark & Purdon, 1995 for a review).

Salkovskis, Forrester and Richards (1998) have assimilated all of this information into a cognitive model (see Figure 5 and Salkovskis, 1999). In essence, it assumes that early experience and critical events at the onset of OCD lead people to hold a set of beliefs or assumptions such as '**not preventing disaster is as bad as causing the disaster**' and '**better to be safe than sorry**'. When an intrusive thought occurs, the person misinterprets the significance of this thought either by believing that the thought predicts behaviour, or believing that they are responsible for preventing an outcome.

Several processes feed into this mechanism. First, OCD sufferers will be on the lookout for obsession-relevant stimuli and may have magical thinking about how they could prevent outcomes (attentional biases). These biases may increase the focus on the original thought (hence loops back to the original obsession). A mood change is also likely to occur (anxiety/depression) which also heightens sensitivity to the original intrusion. Counterproductive strategies such as trying to suppress the thought will increase its frequency. Finally a ritual is engaged in to reduce anxiety, but it actually reinforces the importance of the event (i.e. reinforces the belief that the person did actually prevent a disaster or bad outcome). The ritual prevents the patient from ever disconfirming that the negative outcome would have happened.

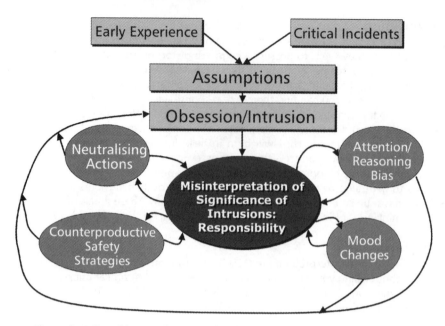

Figure 5: Salkovskis, Forrester & Richards' (1998) cognitive model of OCD
(see Salkovskis, 1999)

Although this model explains the process very well it still doesn't tell us why some people develop the disorder while others don't—by what mechanism does OCD develop? Perhaps then some people have physical abnormalities that contribute to these cognitive processes.

Biological explanations of OCD

If there are qualitative differences in frequency or severity of intrusive thoughts in OCD sufferers then perhaps these differences have their origin in our biological make-up. Biological explanations are in their infancy really, but they tend to focus on a system in the frontal lobe that deals with primitive impulses such as sex, aggression and body excretion. The system is made up of three main structures. The first is the **orbital region of the frontal cortex**, which is the area of the cortex from which these primitive impulses derive (i.e. 'I want to eat', 'I want to drink', 'I want to have sex'). These impulses then travel to an area of the **basal ganglia** called the **caudate nucleus**. This area acts as a sort of filter: it filters out weak impulses and allows only the strongest impulses to reach the third structure, called the **thalamus** (see Chapter 2). If an impulse reaches the thalamus, the person is likely to be motivated to act upon, or think about the impulse more. The action could involve a set of stereotyped behaviours (such as finding food) and once an action is carried out the impulse diminishes.

The biological explanation of OCD supposes that people with this disorder have a brain deficit such that either the initial impulses cannot be switched off, or the impulse can be switched off but the stereotyped behaviours triggered by it cannot (a bit like a record or CD that gets stuck). Support for this idea comes from brain scans that show greater activity in these brain areas in OCD patients compared to normal controls (Baxter et al., 1990) and from evidence that serotonin (which is one of the neurotransmitters in this system) can help OCD symptoms. However, the big problem with this model is that it doesn't explain where the rituals come from (it might explain primitive rituals such as washing, but doesn't really explain more bizarre behaviours such as tapping a window 17 times before entering a house, or counting sequences of numbers).

Quick test

1. How does two-factor theory attempt to explain OCD?

2. How do thought processes in OCD differ from everyday experiences?

3. What is the role of the basal ganglia in OCD?

Section 3

How do we treat OCD?

Although causal theories of how OCD develops are relatively sparse, treatments of the disorder have been rapidly developing. This section looks at how drugs and cognitive therapies can be applied to OCD. During this section you might want to ask yourself to what extent the therapy is getting at the cause of the disorder or the maintaining factors, and whether this distinction matters for long-term clinical benefit.

How therapy works

CRUCIAL CONCEPTS

Exposure and response prevention (ERP) is the treatment of OCD through a combination of the sufferer deliberately eliciting their obsessive thoughts and preventing their associated compulsion.

Drugs

Recent antidepressants (see Chapter 8 for more details of how these drugs work) such as fluoxetine (Prozac) and clomipramine (Anafranil) reduce OCD symptoms in 50-80% of sufferers (Jenike, 1993a, b). Presumably this is because they increase the functional level of serotonin in the frontal lobe.

Exposure and response prevention (ERP)

Many variants on cognitive and behavioural techniques have been used and are based on the idea of exposure to the obsessions (to extinguish anxiety) and prevention of ritualistic behaviours. These therapies have limited effect. Recent advances point towards therapies that employ a variety of cognitive techniques. In brief, therapy hinges on the patient understanding that the key issue is one of worry and not insanity. So OCD patients are worried that if they think about something, for example abusing children, then this means that they will act upon it (e.g. they are a child molester). Early stages of therapy centre on demonstrating that the obsessions could reflect one of two things: in this example, the person actually *is* a child molester, or the person is *worried* about being a child molester. Reframing the problem in this way focuses patients on reducing their worry and reassures them of their normality.

Normalising: part of the therapeutic process involves showing patients that intrusive thoughts are part of everyday life. For example, you can show them that positive intrusions happen regularly (good or creative ideas often pop into our heads), and showing them that situations exist in which negative intrusions could be a good thing (e.g. warning of a potential danger such as being run over by a bus). Finally, patients can be shown that even positive thoughts can be bad in certain contexts (e.g. thinking about laughing with your friends would be inappropriate at a funeral).

Thought–action fusion: the assumption that thought predicts action can be challenged with behavioural experiments. For example, getting patients to think themselves to death (or think the therapist to death) demonstrates how we can have thoughts that do not

71

indicate a future event (of course the therapist has to be careful not to accidentally die at the wrong moment or this would be very counter-productive!). Using these experiments as homework and keeping track of the cognitive processes it elicits can be useful in helping patients reappraise their responsibility over events.

Neutralising: it is important to stop patients using neutralising strategies such as thought suppression. Behavioural experiments can be set up in which you ask patients not to think about something (like earlier on when I suggested you tried not to think about the devil) and this should illustrate to them how trying to suppress thoughts actually increases the frequency of those thoughts. Also, you can set them tasks in which they sometimes try to stop thoughts and sometimes do not and then record thought frequencies. They should find intrusions diminish when suppression is not used and this should provide motivation for stopping these cognitive strategies.

Audio cued exposure: a final technique is to tape obsessions and then play back this tape (in therapy and as homework) to deliberately trigger intrusions. Once triggered, patients are taught to reappraise these thoughts using the strategies already mentioned. This combined exposure to the obsessions and self-reappraisal is a powerful tool in reducing anxiety and providing practice of reappraisal strategies for after therapy.

Not a lot is known about the efficacy of this therapy (it is still relatively new) but earlier versions showed significant improvements in 60-90% of OCD sufferers (Fals-Stewart, Marks & Schafer, 1992) and can last up to six years (Foa & Kozak, 1993). Although it is often reported that CBT has no effect for a substantial minority of sufferers, Warren and Thomas (2001) recently reported that around 84% respond to this form of therapy in routine clinical practice.

Quick test

1. Can drugs be used to treat OCD?

2. What is exposure and response prevention?

3. What techniques have been developed to treat the cognitive aspects of OCD?

Section 4

End of chapter assessment

Questions

1. What is the difference between an obsession and a compulsion?

2. Is OCD learnt or innate?

3. Do people with OCD think differently from people without the disorder?

4. How can we treat OCD and are these treatments effective?

Section 5

Further reading

Salkovskis, P. M., & Kirk, J. (1997). Obsessive-compulsive disorder. In D. M. Clark and C. G. Fairburn (Eds.), *Science and Practice of Cognitive Behaviour Therapy*. Oxford: Oxford

University Press (pp. 179–208). (This is an up-to-date chapter that provides a great review of recent developments in theory and therapy.)

Salkovskis, P. M., & Kirk, J. (1989). Obsessional disorders. In K. Hawton, P. M. Salkovskis, J. Kirk, and D. M. Clark (Eds.), *Cognitive Behaviour Therapy for Psychiatric Problems: A Practical Guide*. Oxford: Oxford University Press (pp. 129–168). (This is a very clear account of how therapy for OCD is put into place.)

Salkovskis, P. M. (1999). Understanding and treating obsessive-compulsive disorder. *Behaviour Research and Therapy*, *37* (July supplement), S29–S52. (This is an excellent overview of current cognitive models of OCD.)

Chapter 7
Eating disorders

Chapter summary

This chapter looks at eating disorders. We begin by seeing how *DSM* defines **anorexia nervosa** and **bulimia nervosa**, before looking at the distinctions between these disorders. The chapter then investigates explanations of these disorders. Little is really known about the causes of eating disorders, and despite some evidence of a genetic component there really isn't compelling evidence that neurotransmitters are involved in the disorders. However, we'll see that learning in the form of vicarious learning and information, as well as classical conditioning, appear to have some role to play. A recent cognitive model is also described that offers a useful framework for future research and treatment. Finally, we'll look at treatments of eating disorders. Drug therapies appear relatively ineffective for anorexia and offer few additional gains to CBT for bulimia, therefore this section mainly describes a CBT approach. The evidence available suggests that this form of therapy is beneficial to the majority of bulimia patients, but virtually nothing is known about its efficacy when applied to anorexia.

Assessment targets

After reading this chapter you should be able to:

Target 1: Explain the key diagnostic criteria for anorexia nervosa and bulimia nervosa. Question 1 at the end of this chapter tests you on this.

Target 2: Explain the biological basis of anorexia nervosa and bulimia nervosa. Question 2 at the end of this chapter tests you on this.

Target 3: Explain the role of learning in the development of anorexia nervosa and bulimia nervosa. Question 3 at the end of this chapter tests you on this.

Target 4: Explain the cognitive model of anorexia nervosa. Question 4 at the end of this chapter tests you on this.

Target 5: Describe how anorexia nervosa and bulimia nervosa are treated and know how successful these treatments are. Question 5 at the end of this chapter tests you on this.

Section 1

What are eating disorders?

This section will look at the differences between how clinical psychologists diagnose anorexia nervosa and bulimia nervosa and explore some of the problems with the diagnostic criteria. You should be familiar with the reasons why accurate diagnosis of disorders is extremely important (see Chapter 1), so while reading this section take note of the differences in the classification of the two disorders and whether you think anorexia and bulimia are reliably distinguished by the diagnostic criteria.

Some background information

Anorexia nervosa is seen by many people as one of the most frustrating psychopathologies and, like bulimia, is seen by some as intractable. According to *DSM* (APA, 1994) both anorexia nervosa and bulimia nervosa are about ten times more likely to occur in women than men. In women the lifetime prevalence of anorexia is estimated to be between 0.5 and 1% and is slightly higher for bulimia nervosa for which estimates range between 1 and 3%. Both disorders typically start in adolescence (the mean onset for anorexia is around 17 years old with peaks at 14 and 18 years old), and often begin after a period of dieting. Anorexia is often precipitated by a stressful life event and bulimics are often slightly overweight before the disorder develops. Both disorders are often accompanied by depression and other disorders such as OCD, phobias and panic (Kennedy & Garfinkel, 1992). Although many psychological disorders do not lead to death, suicide rates are higher in both anorexics and bulimics compared to the general population. Both disorders can be fatal for reasons other than suicide (10% of anorexics die from the disorder), the most common causes of death are starvation or physical complications such as congestive heart failure or electrolyte imbalance. The terminal nature of these disorders makes them a major challenge for modern clinical psychology.

Diagnosis of anorexia nervosa

Anorexia nervosa is actually an entirely inappropriate name as it literally means a nervous (nervosa) loss of appetite (anorexia). In fact anorexics, far from losing their appetite, become preoccupied with food. The disorder is characterised by an intense fear of weight gain even though underweight, and cognitive disturbances about one's body shape.

CRUCIAL DIAGNOSIS

DSM-IV characterises anorexia nervosa as follows:

A. Refusal to maintain body weight at or above a minimally normal weight for age and height (e.g., weight loss leading to maintenance of body weight less than 85% of that expected; or failure to make expected weight gain during period of growth, leading to body weight less than 85% of that expected).

B. Intense fear of gaining weight or becoming fat, even though underweight.

C. Disturbance in the way in which one's body weight or shape is experienced, undue influence of body weight or shape on self-evaluation, or denial of the seriousness of the current low body weight.

D. In postmenarcheal females, amenorrhoea, i.e. the absence of at least three consecutive menstrual cycles. (A woman is considered to have amenorrhoea if her periods occur only following hormone, e.g., estrogen, administration.)

DSM-IV also recognises two distinct subtypes of anorexia. The main difference between these subtypes is whether the person engages in **binge-eating** and **purging** behaviours.

- In the **binge-eating/purging** type of anorexia the person has to regularly engage in binge-eating or purging behaviour during their current anorexic episode. Binge-eating is the consumption of abnormal amounts of food in a short space of time and purging is self-induced vomiting or the misuse of laxatives, diuretics or enemas (see diagnosis of bulimia nervosa below).

- The second subtype is **restricting type** anorexia, in which the person does not regularly engage in the binge-eating or purging behaviour described previously during their current episode of anorexia.

The key parts of these diagnostic criteria are that the person has a cognitive disturbance in the way that they view their own body shape, and that they have an intense fear of gaining weight.

─────────── CRUCIAL CASE STUDY ───────────

Clare's mum noticed that Clare had stopped having periods and that for nearly a year now her weight had been steadily dropping. What her mother didn't realise was that Clare had started to restrict her eating because she found herself preoccupied with her body weight and calorific intake. In particular, she hated the shape of her bum and thighs, and was intensely fearful of gaining weight. Although, objectively, her body shape was normal, Clare's perception of herself was completely distorted and she began to exercise profusely to try to achieve the body shape that she wanted. Clare remembers beginning to worry about her appearance after being bullied in school. She now has very low self-esteem and often contemplates killing herself. Recently she had begun to induce vomiting after eating.

Diagnosis of bulimia nervosa

The word bulimia comes from a Greek word meaning 'ox hunger', and again 'nervosa' implicates a nervous disorder. This name makes more sense when you understand that the disorder is characterised by episodes of rapidly eating huge amounts of food. This consumption is almost invariably followed by behaviours to prevent weight gain, such as vomiting, fasting or excessive exercise.

─────────── CRUCIAL DIAGNOSIS ───────────

The *Diagnostic and Statistical Manual of Mental Disorders* (*DSM-IV*) characterises bulimia nervosa as follows:

A. Recurrent episodes of binge-eating. An episode of binge-eating is characterised by both of the following:

1) Eating, in a discrete period of time (e.g., within any two-hour period), an amount of food that is definitely larger than most people would eat during a similar period of time and under similar circumstances.
2) A sense of lack of control over eating during the episode (e.g., a feeling that one cannot stop eating or control what or how much one is eating).

B. Recurrent inappropriate compensatory behaviour in order to prevent weight gain, such as self-induced vomiting; misuse of laxatives, diuretics, enemas or other medications; fasting; or excessive exercise.

C. The binge-eating and inappropriate compensatory behaviours both occur, on average, at least twice a week for three months.

D. Self-evaluation is unduly influenced by body shape and weight.

E. The disturbance does not occur exclusively during episodes of anorexia nervosa.

There are two subtypes of bulimia that *DSM-IV* recognises, these subtypes differ mainly in the form of the compensatory behaviour. In **purging type** bulimia, the person has to have regularly engaged in self-induced vomiting or the misuse of laxatives, diuretics or enemas during their current episode of bulimia. In **nonpurging type bulimia** the person has to have used non-purging compensatory behaviours such as fasting or excessive exercise, but must not have regularly engaged in the purging behaviour described above.

The main aspects of this disorder are that the person engages in binge-eating, and that they feel a lack of control over their eating. The second key thing is that the person engages in behaviours to prevent weight gain (either by purging, or through exercise). This binge-eating and purging is almost always associated with extreme feelings of guilt and shame. Bulimia is sometimes triggered by a period of dieting in which the patient 'lapses' and eats 'forbidden foods', and then induces vomiting to compensate for this lapse. Bulimics often also have a history of comfort eating, in which food is used as a means to reduce unhappiness, anxiety or depression.

Differences between anorexia nervosa and bulimia nervosa

On the face of it anorexia and bulimia seem like similar disorders. In fact Bulimia has been recognised as a separate diagnostic category only since the 1970s. The two disorders are not mutually exclusive, with *DSM-IV* readily recognising that many anorexics engage in bulimic behaviours (hence the binge-eating/purging subtype). If you look at the diagnostic criteria, there are many points of crossover: both disorders are characterised by self-evaluation that is focused on body shape and physical appearance, both disorders involve some kind of control of eating either through binge-eating and purging, or excessive exercise or use of laxatives (in both disorders). In many ways this raises questions about the distinctiveness of the disorders and whether it is useful to distinguish them. However, there are some core differences, which at least appear to be useful points of demarcation for treatment. Whether it turns out that these demarcations are useful in building predictive causal models of the disorders remains to be seen.

The first point of departure is in terms of body weight. One key aspect of anorexia is that sufferers refuse to maintain a normal body weight for their build and height (in fact they have to be 15% below), bulimics on the other hand tend to maintain average body weights for their height and build. In addition, anorexics have distortions about their body image, which bulimics do not experience—at least according to the diagnostic criteria (although Cooper and Fairburn, 1993, have pointed out that many bulimics idealise a thin body shape and feel that their own body is repulsive and overweight). A second point of departure is that a diagnosis of bulimia requires that binge-eating and compensatory behaviours occur at least twice a week for three months. Like many other disorders, this shows a reliance on arbitrary cut-off points; look back at Chapters 3–6 and on to Chapter 8 and you'll see most diagnostic criteria have some kind of arbitrary cut-off incorporated in it somewhere and I discuss the problems with these in most of these chapters (especially Chapter 8). It's probably not realistic to use a cut-off of binge-eating and vomiting twice a week because Garfinkel, Kennedy and Kaplan (1995) have found that there are a few differences between those who engage in these behaviours less than twice a week and those who engage in them more than twice a week. If this criterion were to be dropped (which is possible in future editions of *DSM*), then there's one less distinction to be made between the disorders. The other possible distinction is in control: although in both disorders control of eating is key, bulimics appear to lack control over their eating whereas restrictive anorexics appear to exert excessive control.

Quick test

1. What are the key diagnostic features of anorexia nervosa?
2. What are the key diagnostic criteria of bulimia nervosa?

Section 2

Can we explain eating disorders?

One of the biggest problems in the field of eating disorders is an absence of a strong theoretical model, based on careful experimental research. Such is the problem that Jansen (2001) recently wrote that '... the effectiveness of treatments for anorexia nervosa in particular is very slight. This is not at all surprising when considering the fact that there is still no explanation for why some people suffer or keep suffering from anorexia nervosa' (p.1008). Jansen goes on to argue that this lack of knowledge has led some clinicians to actually believe that there are simply an infinite number of causes of eating disorders.

CRUCIAL CONCEPT

The **multicausality model** is the idea that there is no central cause of eating disorders, but that they simply arise from any number of biological, social or psychological factors that may vary from individual to individual.

The multicausality model is particularly unhelpful because in essence it suggests that eating disorders arise from any number of factors that can differ from person to person, and that the co-occurrence of any identical set of these factors may give rise to a disorder in one person but not another. In theoretical terms this means that there is no way to make predictions about when or why an eating disorder will develop. The basic premise of science is to unearth causal mechanisms: if we cannot make causal attributions then, in effect, we know nothing useful about the topic we're studying (Field & Hole, 2002). The multicausality model suggests that there's no point in even *trying* to explain eating disorders. Equally as disturbing, it implies that a common treatment model cannot be formulated: treatment should be unique for every person because the cause of their particular problem will be different from everyone else's! Although this is a frequently accepted position (see Jansen, 2001), is there any evidence that this is in fact the case? This section looks at some of what we do know about common processes in eating disorders and presents some attempts to make predictions about when and why eating disorders develop.

Biological factors

Studies of eating disorders in female twins have revealed a concordance rate for bulimia (Kendler, MacLean, Neale & Kessler, 1991) of 23% in monozygotic twins (these are twins from the same egg and so are genetically identical) compared to 9% in dizygotic twins (these are twins from different eggs and so share an average of only 50% of their genes). In anorexia, around 56% of monozygotic twins both end up with eating disorders compared to only 5% in dizygotic twins (Holland, Hall, Murray, Russell & Crisp, 1984). Also, first-degree relatives of women with eating disorders are four times more likely than average to have an eating disorder themselves (Strober, Lampert, Morrell, Burroughs, & Jacobs, 1990). This evidence suggests a genetic factor in eating disorders.

If there is a genetic link, then this link may be through brain functioning. We saw in Chapter 2 that one area of the brain that plays an important role in basic biological functions (like eating) is the hypothalamus. Although damage to the hypothalamus in animals does lead to loss of appetite and weight loss (Hoebel & Tietelbaum, 1966), this is rather different from the experience of anorexics who do not lose their appetite but restrict food intake anyway. However, the neurotransmitter serotonin (which operates in the limbic system which is closely associated with the hypothalamus – see Chapter 2) does seem to influence food intake; levels of serotonin are low in underweight individuals with anorexia nervosa but then rise to above normal levels in individuals who have made longstanding recoveries (Jimerson, Lesem, Kaye, Hegg & Brewerton, 1990; Kaye, Gwirtsman, George & Ebert, 1991). It is therefore possible that a disturbance in serotonin levels might be a risk factor for developing anorexia. Bulimics also appear to have low levels of serotonin (Jimerson et al., 1997; Mitchell & deZwaan, 1993) and norepinephrine (Fava, Copeland, Schweiger, & Herzog, 1989), which also acts in the limbic system. As with anorexia, levels of serotonin return to normal or above normal after recovery (Wolfe et al., 2000; Kaye, Greeno, Moss, Fernstrom & Fernstrom, 1998).

However, as Walsh and Devlin (1998) point out, these kinds of findings fall well short of establishing a causal link between biological aberrations and eating disorders. The main problem is that most of these physiological disturbances resolve when body weight returns to normal and this suggests that they don't have a role as etiological factors. Therefore this evidence needs to be viewed cautiously because it's likely that the disorder causes the biological problems not vice versa.

The role of learning

Although there isn't a formal learning theory of eating disorders, learning clearly contributes to the process. Earlier in this chapter we saw that body dissatisfaction is a core factor in the aetiology and maintenance of eating disorder (see Polivy & Herman, 2002). This body dissatisfaction stems from negative evaluations of body shapes perceived to be even marginally overweight. These negative evaluations are likely to have many sources such as exposure to idealised thin media images (Russell, 1992), peer pressure and maternal influence (Stice, 1998; Levine, Smolak, Moodey, Shuman & Hessen, 1994), and teasing (Lunner et al., 2000). All of these processes are likely to involve vicarious learning or exposure to negative information about overweight body shapes; we saw in Chapter 3 how these types of learning can translate into fear and anxiety. However, learning processes may have a further role to play. Lascelles, Field and Davey (in press) have suggested that if perceptions of one's own or others' body shapes can acquire negative affect through such a variety of sources, then it is possible that this negative perception of certain body shapes might become associated with either food or the eating of food, and consequently lead to negative perceptions of food. They suggest that classical conditioning (see Chapter 3) is a plausible mechanism through which food may become associated with weight gain and distorted body image (Cooper & Fairburn, 1992; Dritschel, Williams & Cooper, 1991). In the first study of its kind, Lascelles et al. used a classical conditioning procedure in which foodstuffs were presented alongside different body shapes. They showed that self-reported attitudes about the foodstuffs became more negative after they were associated with disliked body-shapes (these were pictures of overweight women). Although more work needs to be done, this study showed that classical conditioning might have a role to play in eating disorders through forming associations between body shapes and foods.

A cognitive model of anorexia

I mentioned earlier on that the area of eating disorder is lacking theoretical insight; however, a model of anorexia has recently been put forward by Christopher Fairburn and his colleagues (Fairburn, Shafran, & Cooper, 1999). Figure 6 shows this model. Fairburn et al. argue that the central feature of eating disorders is an extreme need to control eating.

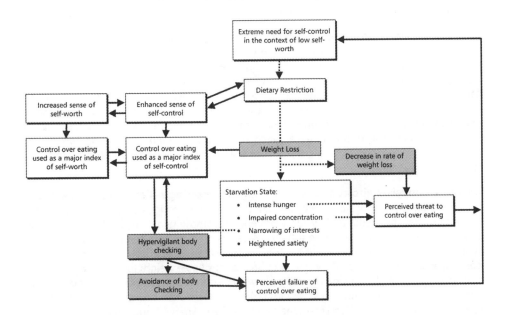

Figure 6: Fairburn, Shafran & Cooper's (1999) model of anorexia nervosa. Shaded boxes are processes specific to Western cases of anorexia and dotted lines are processes that develop over an extended time.

Initially this need for control stems from the interaction between the individual's characteristic sense of ineffectiveness and perfectionism, and some longstanding low self-esteem (Vitousek and Manke, 1994; Bruch, 1973). At first, they argue, individuals may experiment with controlling various aspects of their life such as work, sport or other interests (Bruch, 1973), but this soon transfers to control over food. The reasons for this transfer are:

- successful dietary restriction provides direct and immediate evidence of self-control because control over eating does not rely on other people (unlike work, sport etc., Slade, 1982);
- controlling eating has a potent effect on significant others, which is important given that there are often pre-existing dysfunctional relationships with these people (Vandereycken, Kog, & Vanderlinden, 1989);
- eating may already be a highly salient behaviour in the family (Kalucy, Crisp, & Harding, 1977);
- controlling eating provides a means of stopping puberty, the onset of which may constitute a threat to self-control (remember that these disorders typically start in adolescence); and
- Western societies promote dieting to control shape and weight, which encourages similar associations to be formed.

Fairburn *et al.*, suggest that once a person begins to restrict eating, this behaviour will be reinforced through three feedback mechanisms; as such, the disorder becomes self-perpetuating. All three mechanisms evolve over time and their relative influence changes from moment to moment.

Dietary restriction enhances the sense of being in control (see Figure 6). I hinted at this above by mentioning Slade's (1982) suggestion that restricting eating directly and immediately enhances an individual's sense of being in control. The initial success at restricting food intake and the consequent sense of self-control reinforces further restriction. Over time, control over eating becomes an index of general self-control and also self-worth. At the same time the person becomes preoccupied with food and so by successfully controlling their eating these individuals control something that is important in their lives and they also avoid other difficulties (e.g. the family, sexual relationships).

Aspects of starvation encourage further dietary restriction (see Figure 6). The weight loss that comes from dietary restriction gives rise to a state of starvation. The psychological and physiological changes associated with this weight loss undermine the person's sense of control (e.g. feeling full, because of a smaller stomach, may be seen as a failure to control eating and intense hunger may be seen as a threat to maintaining control). Starvation also impairs concentration, which makes people prone to perceive events as unpredictable and uncontrollable. This further undermines the person's sense of control. Starvation also promotes a preoccupation with food and eating which will exaggerate the tendency to use control over eating as an index of self-control and self-worth (see above).

Extreme concerns about shape and weight encourage dietary restriction. This final mechanism is specific to Western cultures. In the previous section on learning, I suggested that the media and cultural influences promote negative views about fatness. Fairburn *et al.* suggest that these influences can contribute to a tendency to judge self-worth in terms of shape and weight. Weight loss is often an anorexic's main index of self-control, and the major goal of food restriction is quantifiable weight loss. As such, sufferers will check their weight for signs of progress with dips in weight being seen as evidence of successful self-control (and hence rewarding) and weight gain being seen as evidence of loss of control (and hence food restriction is intensified). Shape change may also be used as an index of self-control, which explains anorexics' tendencies to become fixated on parts of their bodies. Fairburn *et al.* suggest that anorexics have confirmatory information processing biases that distort body-shape data, so perceived bodily imperfections are magnified by frequent checking of shape while in a state of high arousal; arousal, self-focused attention and anxiety will increase also, which creates a vicious circle by encouraging further monitoring. Put simply, anorexics come to think that they are failing to control their shape (by their high standards) and so persist with their dietary restriction.

This model is certainly a massive step in the right direction (especially in terms of developing common treatment tools of eating disorders). However, we're still at the stage where a lot more research needs to be done to see whether these processes actually cause anorexia, or whether they merely describe the end state of the disorder. This model does, though, provide a useful framework in which research can be conducted.

Quick test

1. Are neurotransmitters responsible for eating disorders?

2. What is the contribution of learning to eating disorders?

3. Describe the cognitive model of anorexia nervosa.

Section 3

How are eating disorders treated?

The final part of this chapter examines different treatments of eating disorders. Jansen (2001) reports that in daily practice, numerous different treatments are employed from psychoanalysis to multimodal treatments; however, only a third of patients receive cognitive behavioural treatment for bulimia nervosa, despite this method being probably the best researched and most efficacious. She claims that in an American study most of the therapists questioned used 'eclectic methods', which she suggested was a euphemism for 'doing what you feel like'. With anorexia, the multicausality model is often used as a therapeutic model; the natural implication from this being that patients are all treated as individuals, with no common ground in treatment terms. Although therapies should allow flexibility for individuals, some common framework is always useful: as Jansen points out, if two people break their leg then both have their leg placed in a cast, regardless of what caused the break.

This section looks primarily at the use of cognitive behavioural therapies for bulimia and anorexia.

Drug therapy

The implication of serotonin and norepinephrine in eating disorders raises the immediate possibility that antidepressants (which act on these neurotransmitters – see Chapter 8) might be an effective treatment. However, these drugs appear to have little therapeutic effect for anorexia (Ferguson, La Via, Crossan & Kaye, 1999; and see Walsh and Devlin, 1998, for a review). Interestingly, the story is somewhat different for bulimia, which according to Walsh and Devlin has been shown to respond to antidepressants in over a dozen well-controlled studies. However, relapse rates are very high when the medication is stopped.

Therapy for bulimia nervosa

Fairburn (1997) describes a therapy for bulimia based on cognitive behavioural techniques. In essence there are three stages to therapy.

Stage 1
In the first stage the emphasis is on presenting a cognitive account of what maintains the

disorder while using behavioural techniques to try to eliminate binge-eating and initiate a pattern of stable eating. The therapist draws up a basic representation of the factors that maintain the disorder and tailor this to specific issues that the patient has raised. The important thing at this stage is to stress that the binge-eating is only part of the problem and that the person's thoughts and feelings about their eating have to be addressed also. There are several important processes:

- **Self-monitoring**: patients are encouraged to monitor their eating (a bit like keeping a structured diary). This helps to identify specific problems and habits.

- **Monitoring body weight**: patients are asked to weigh themselves once a week on a day of their choice. The main purpose of this is that it becomes important in subsequent behavioural experiments.

- **Education**: this is the most important part of this stage and consists of the therapist discussing various aspects of eating with the patient. This is largely aimed at overcoming misconceptions. The topics covered are: body weight and its regulation, the physical effects of binge-eating, the ineffectiveness of vomiting, laxatives and diuretics as a means of weight control, and the effects of dieting. The therapist also prescribes a pattern of regular eating (three planned meals a day and two to three planned snacks). These meals should not be followed by compensatory behaviours, and there shouldn't be more than a three-hour gap between meals. This all needs strong emphasis because it is aimed at replacing the binge/restrain pattern associated with the disorder. Simultaneously, the therapist isolates behaviours that can be used to displace or delay binges (such as exercise, taking a shower, or phoning a friend). The patient is encouraged to engage in these behaviours whenever the temptation to binge arises. Finally, patients are advised not to vomit (and if this cannot be easily done they can be encouraged to eat only things that they are prepared not to vomit) and to throw away any laxatives or diuretics and to cease using them.

- **Interviewing key friends and relatives**: towards the end of stage one the therapist should attempt to bring in some friends and relatives to bring the problem into the open, to check that the patient has understood the principles of therapy and to provide an educated environment for the patient.

Stage 2

This stage of therapy continues the emphasis on regular eating and use of alternative behaviours to displace binges. In addition, some of the core cognitive difficulties are also addressed:

- **Dieting**: a major goal of therapy is to reduce the tendency of these people to diet. First, foods that are avoided are identified (perhaps by asking patients to go to a supermarket and to write down anything they wouldn't eat because of its effect on weight and body shape). These foods are then slowly introduced into the regular meals and snacks (in amounts that the person feels comfortable with). To overcome restriction of the total amount eaten, patients are encouraged to eat at least 1,500 kcals per day if they are not doing so. Patients who are calorie-conscious should be encouraged to relax controls over eating (such as eating meals of unknown calorie content).

- **Problem-solving**: once the patient is binge-eating intermittently rather than regularly, specific episodes of binging should be identified, and problem-solving skills taught (by perhaps identifying the things that trigger these occasional binges).

- **Concerns about shape and weight**: cognitive restructuring is used here (see Chapter 8) in conjunction with behavioural techniques to address concerns about shape and weight. Patients are encouraged to note down thoughts that contribute to the problem as they happen, these thoughts can then be addressed in therapy. Arguments or evidence to support the thought should be marshalled (e.g. if the patient has gained weight this does not support the thought 'I am fat'). Conversely, arguments or evidence to contradict the thought should be identified. Care needs to be taken here to take account of what the thought means to the patient. For example, the thought 'I am fat' is somewhat different from the person feeling as though they are fat (but not literally thinking that they are). Thoughts can be challenged using Socratic questioning (e.g. 'what constitutes fat?' 'what size of clothes would a fat person wear?' 'does the fact you've gained weight mean you are approaching that clothes size?'). Finally, patients should reach a reasonable conclusion about the thought in question (even if they don't necessarily believe that conclusion).

- **General attitudes**: a similar approach is taken to general attitudes that may contribute to the problem. For example, someone might believe that reaching an ideal weight will 'solve all of their problems'. By identifying this attitude, collecting evidence against it, and qualifying dysfunctional evidence for it, the patient should be able to reach a reasonable conclusion about whether the attitude is realistic.

- **Behavioural experiments**: bulimics will often take opportunities to avoid showing their body (for example, by wearing baggy clothes). Behavioural experiments can be employed in which the patient is encouraged to show more of their body, through wearing tighter clothes or going swimming. If patients have the opposite problem and over-scrutinise their body, then they should be encouraged to identify a woman (assuming the patient is female) who they deem as beautiful, and then identify her imperfections (which, although it sounds a bit nasty to the poor observed woman, will show the patient that even the most attractive of women have imperfections, cellulite etc.).

Stage 3

Consists entirely of relapse prevention. The most important part of this is to reassure patients that it is unrealistic for them to expect never to binge again. They should be told that relapse is likely, but reminded of the skills they have learned to help them get over these setbacks.

Therapy for anorexia nervosa

There isn't nearly such a well-developed and formal therapy for anorexia (although developments such as Fairburn *et al.*'s model should move things on in the near future). Fairburn (1997) suggests that the therapy just outlined for bulimia should be easily applied to anorexia. However, he suggests two modifications:

Motivation to change: most anorexics are extremely reluctant to accept their diagnosis, let alone change. Fairburn emphasises the importance of the therapeutic relationship for motivating the patient to change. It is important that the patient realises that the therapist is working to help them (and is not some agent working on behalf of concerned relatives, for example). Most important is that the therapist helps the patient look to the long-term gains of therapy and not focus on short-term issues (which they tend to do). Fairburn also suggests getting the patient to read accessible books about the disorder (in particular he mentions Palmer, 1988), which helps them to accept the diagnosis (as they come to see similarities between themselves and the patients described in the books).

Restoring healthy weight: weight loss is obviously a major concern in therapy for anorexia. According to Fairburn, it is important to first establish a good therapeutic relationship, after which weight gain should become a non-negotiable part of therapy. A target should be set (Fairburn suggests a target weight range somewhere above a BMI of 19). Weight gain should be gradual (1kg a week being a reasonable target) and should be obtained either through high calorific foods or energy-rich drink supplements (which some patients find easier to take because they can view them as 'medicine'). The use of high-energy drinks should be stopped once the target weight has been achieved and the patient needs to be encouraged to maintain weight through eating food, rather than drink supplements. Once a healthy body weight has been obtained, therapy can continue as for bulimia.

CRUCIAL CONCEPT

The **body mass index (BMI)** is a measure of the ratio of a person's height to their weight. The actual equation is:

$$BMI = \frac{\text{weight in kilograms}}{(\text{height in metres})^2}$$

A normal range for this index is between 20 and 25; as values rise above this range this indicates a progressive tendency towards being above a healthy weight for your height, conversely, values below this range indicate being underweight. Typically, anorexics have a BMI below 17.

How successful is therapy?

In terms of bulimia nervosa, Craighead and Argus (1991) found an average reduction in the frequency of purging of 79% when pooling the results of ten controlled studies using cognitive behavioural techniques. Similarly, Wilson (1996) looked at eight subsequent studies and found a mean reduction of 86%. Across all of these 18 studies, around 56% of patients completely abstained from purging after therapy. These gains appear to be well maintained, with Fairburn et al. (1995) reporting that 63% of patients had no eating disorder an average of six months after therapy. Wilson (1996) reported that the addition of antidepressant medication resulted in no additional benefit above and beyond that of cognitive behavioural therapy.

Much less is known about the efficacy of CBT for anorexia. One study does exist (Channon, de Silva, Hemsley, & Perkins, 1989), but this included a relatively small number of patients and did not follow a rigid treatment programme (none existed at the time) so it tells us little about the success of modern therapies like those outlined by Fairburn (1997) and summarised in this chapter.

Quick test

1. Are drugs an effective way to treat eating disorders?
2. Describe a typical treatment of bulimia nervosa.
3. What unique therapeutic approaches need to be taken when treating anorexia nervosa?

Section 4

End of chapter assessment

Questions

1. What is anorexia nervosa and how does it differ from bulimia nervosa?
2. Do bulimia nervosa and anorexia nervosa have a biological basis?
3. Are eating disorders learnt?
4. How do dysfunctional beliefs contribute to the onset and maintenance of anorexia nervosa?
5. What are the similarities (and differences) in the treatment of bulimia nervosa and anorexia nervosa? How successful are these treatments?

Section 5

Further reading

Fairburn, C. G. (1997). Eating disorders. In D. M. Clark and C. G. Fairburn (Eds.), *Science and Practice of Cognitive Behaviour Therapy* (pp. 209–241). Oxford: Oxford University Press. (An excellent overview of therapy for eating disorders.)

Fairburn, C. G., Shafran, R. & Cooper, Z. (1999) A cognitive behavioural theory of anorexia nervosa. *Behaviour Research and Therapy,* 37, 1–13. (This paper outlines the cognitive model of eating disorders.)

Palmer, J. L. (1988). *Anorexia nervosa*. London: Penguin. (An old, but nevertheless helpful, introduction to anorexia.)

Chapter 8
Depression

Chapter summary

This chapter examines what's been termed the 'common cold of psychiatry': **depression**. There are many different types of depression and this chapter begins by looking at the difference between the two major types: **major depressive disorder** and **bipolar depression**. We then look at the many different subtypes of depression, which can differ in terms of the trigger (seasonal, childbirth) or unusual symptoms (e.g. hallucinations), or particular clusters of depressive symptoms (e.g. atypical depression). We then move on to look at explanations of depression and we begin with Beck's model of depression, which suggests that negative early experiences lead people to develop a set of negative schemata about themselves and the world. These negative schemata are triggered by critical life incidents and, once activated, lead to a stream of negative automatic thoughts and misinterpretations. A second theory that we look at is learned helplessness theory, which explains depression in terms of people learning that they have no control over their lives. The final explanation we explore is that depressive symptoms are caused by low levels of serotonin in the brain (especially the limbic system). We conclude the chapter by looking at how depression is treated, first by exploring various antidepressants (TCAs, MAOIs, SSRIs, SNRIs) and then examining cognitive behaviour therapy.

Assessment targets

After reading this chapter you should be able to:

Target 1: **Explain the key diagnostic criteria for depression. Question 1 at the end of this chapter tests you on this.**

Target 2: **Explain the differences between subtypes of depression. Question 2 at the end of this chapter tests you on this.**

Target 3: **Describe Beck's cognitive model of depression. Question 3 at the end of this chapter tests you on this.**

Target 4: **Explain learned helplessness. Question 4 at the end of this chapter tests you on this.**

Target 5: **Understand the role of serotonin in depression. Question 5 at the end of this chapter tests you on this.**

Target 6: **Explain how depression is treated and relate the therapies back to the theories on which they are based. Question 6 at the end of this chapter tests you on this.**

Section 1

What is depression?

Most of us know what it's like to 'be depressed': we have all experienced negative mood states in which we ruminate about negative themes, feel the need for reassurance, brood about unpleasant events and feel pessimistic about the future. However, for some people these common feelings become more severe, drawing in extreme emotional responses (hopelessness and despair), cognitive changes (low self-esteem, guilt, memory biases, and difficulty concentrating), and behavioural (reduced motivation, loss of interest in usually pleasurable activities) and physical (inability to sleep, sexual dysfunction, energy loss) changes. At any one time around 5% of the population are suffering from a clinical level of depression and 15–39% of these episodes continue to one year; in nearly a quarter of cases the depression takes a chronic course (see Williams, 1997). Women are about twice as likely as men to suffer from depression. This section looks at how depression is diagnosed, and the different subtypes of depression.

Diagnosis of depression

CRUCIAL CONCEPT

There are two main types of depression: **major depressive disorder** (unipolar depression) and **bipolar depression** (what used to be called manic depression). These two types are distinguished by the presence of manic episodes: major depressive disorder consists of only depressive episodes, whereas in manic depression the patient cycles between major depression and manic episodes.

Major depressive disorder (which you'll sometimes find called unipolar depression) is defined solely in terms of a major depressive episode (there must be no mania). These episodes are defined in terms of a list of symptoms; sufferers must experience five of these symptoms within the same two-week period to be classified as having a major depressive episode.

CRUCIAL DIAGNOSIS

The *Diagnostic and Statistical Manual of Mental Disorders* (DSM-IV) characterises a major depressive episode as follows:

A. Five or more of the following in the past two weeks:
  - depressed mood most of the day, nearly every day, as indicated by self-report or observations by others;
  - markedly diminished interest or pleasure in all, or almost all, activities most of the day, nearly every day;
  - significant weight loss when not dieting, or weight gain, or decrease or increase in appetite nearly every day;
  - insomnia (inability to fall asleep, or inability to fall back to sleep after waking in the middle of the night, or waking early) or hypersomnia (desire to stay in bed for large portions of the day);
  - psychomotor agitation or retardation (lethargy);
  - fatigue or loss of energy;
  - feelings of worthlessness, excessive or inappropriate guilt;
  - diminished ability to think or concentrate, or indecisiveness;
  - recurrent thoughts of death, suicidal ideation, or suicide attempt.

B. Not a mixed episode: a mixed episode is a depressive episode (as defined by the five symptoms) occurring at the same time as a manic episode (described later). These mixed episodes do not count as major depression.

C. Symptoms cause significant distress or impairment of functioning: As ever, *DSM* specifies that the symptoms experienced must impair social or occupational functioning. The degree of impairment necessary is not defined.

D. Not due to substance abuse/medical condition: depression is especially linked with alcohol abuse and this appears to be a reciprocal relationship.

E. Not better explained by bereavement: depression after bereavement is very common and so this does not count as a depressive episode (because it reflects the 'normal' grieving process and not a psychiatric disorder).

F. Episodes are not better accounted for by another disorder: as always, *DSM* covers itself by saying that the symptoms with which the patient presents should not be better explained by another diagnosis.

G. There has never been a manic episode: this criterion is to separate unipolar and bipolar depression. Manic episodes should occur only in bipolar depression.

An important issue here is the criterion of five of these symptoms within a two-week period. It isn't at all clear whether someone with five of these symptoms in a two-week period differs from someone who experiences four of these symptoms for two weeks, or from someone who has all five symptoms but for only ten days. The cut-off values imposed by the classification system seem somewhat arbitrary. Again, this is where a clinician would be expected to use their clinical judgement. One of the other key diagnostic features is the absence of any manic or mixed episodes. This is to distinguish major depressive disorder from bipolar depression, in which sufferers experience depressive episodes as described before, but also have periods of mania. To understand why this distinction is made, we should first look at what a manic episode actually is.

CRUCIAL DIAGNOSIS

DSM-IV defines mania as a distinct period of abnormally and persistently elevated, expansive or irritable mood lasting at least one week. Again, the criterion of lasting a week seems somewhat arbitrary (if it lasts six days is it not mania?). The manic episode is again defined in terms of a symptom checklist:

A. Three or more of the following symptoms:
- inflated self-esteem or grandiosity;
- decreased need for sleep;
- more talkative than usual;
- flight of ideas or the subjective feeling of racing thoughts;
- distractibility;
- increased goal-directed activity or psychomotor agitation;
- excessive involvement in pleasurable activities that have a high potential for painful consequences (e.g. spending vast amounts of money, hedonism).

B. Not a mixed episode: as with unipolar depression this manic episode should not coincide with a depressive one (in bipolar disorder the depressive and manic episodes occur sequentially not concurrently).

C. Symptoms cause significant distress or impairment of functioning: as ever, *DSM* specifies that the symptoms experienced must impair social or occupational functioning. The degree of impairment necessary is, again, not explicitly defined.

D. Not due to substance abuse/medical condition: depression is especially linked with alcohol abuse and this appears to be a reciprocal relationship.

Major subtypes of depression

Major depressive disorder and bipolar depression can be divided into several subtypes. Major depressive disorder can be divided into major depressive disorder (already described) and a milder but more chronic form known as **dysthymic disorder**. Dysthymic disorder is diagnosed by having depressed mood in addition to two other symptoms from the list for major depressive disorder for at least two years. Within these two years, the person must not have been free of these symptoms for more than a two-month period. It is also possible to experience both major depressive disorder and dysthymic disorder. This is known as **double depression** and is characterised by chronic mild depressive symptoms that peak into major depressive episodes but never recover to normal levels (merely return to the mild depressive state).

Likewise, bipolar depression has a milder form known as cyclothymic disorder in which sufferers alternate between manic and depressive states both of which are milder than full-blown mania or depressive episodes. However, these states are chronic with the person alternating between mania and depression for at least a two-year period. Typically the manic periods do not hinder everyday life, but the depressive episodes do.

CRUCIAL TIP

Bipolar disorder can be split into two categories: **bipolar I disorder**, in which full mania is experienced, and **bipolar II disorder**, in which severe depression is experienced but with milder manic episodes (these milder manic episodes are called **hypomania**).

Table 1 shows the subtypes of depression that I've described so far. However, within each of these subtypes there are further distinctions that can be made. These subtypes are all associated with major depressive disorder but are selectively associated with the depressive and manic episodes in bipolar disorder (see Table 1).

Major Depressive Disorder	Bipolar Disorder	
Dysthymic Disorder	**Cyclothymic Disorder**	
	Depression	**Mania**
Melancholic	Melancholic	Psychotic
Atypical	Atypical	Catatonic
Psychotic		Postpartum
Catatonic		Seasonal onset
Postpartum		
Seasonal onset		

Table 1: Subtypes of depression

Depression with melancholic features

This form of depression is thought to be purely biologically based, and is characterised by a distinct inability to experience pleasure. In addition, sufferers must have at least three of the following symptoms:

- distinct quality of depressed mood;
- depression that is regularly worse in the mornings;
- early waking;
- significant anorexia or weight loss;
- marked psychomotor agitation or retardation; or
- excessive or inappropriate guilt.

Depression with atypical features

This subtype is defined in terms of the sufferer experiencing positive mood reactions to positive events, but with at least two of the following four features:

- weight gain or increased appetite;
- hypersomnia (sleeping ten hours or more per day);
- feelings of heavy limbs; and
- a long-standing over-sensitivity to interpersonal rejection.

Depression with psychotic features

In this subtype, the sufferer experiences delusions and hallucinations during depressive episodes (see Chapter 9 on schizophrenia for definitions of these symptoms). Typically the delusions and hallucinations are very negative and could be things like a belief that they are an evil person, or hearing voices that accuse them of terrible acts.

Depression with catatonic features

This form of depression is accompanied by catatonic behaviour (again, see Chapter 9 for descriptions of catatonia).

Depression with postpartum features

This is known colloquially as post-natal depression and should be distinguished from postpartum blues. Around 30% of women experience postpartum blues, which involves rapidly changing moods, irritability and crying for no reason after childbirth. However, these feelings last only a few weeks and are typically annoying rather than life-changing. Postpartum depression must occur within four weeks of childbirth and should meet the full criteria for a depressive episode.

Depression with seasonal onset

Formerly known as **seasonal affective disorder** (**SAD**) this form of depression has its onset in periods of low levels of daylight (in the northern hemisphere this would be between October–February). People with this disorder sometimes develop mania during summer periods when the daylight hours are at their longest.

Problems with the diagnosis

I've already mentioned that the classification system relies on some fairly arbitrary decisions about the number of symptoms and the duration of those symptoms. In addition, some of the sub-types are difficult to distinguish from the main disorder, for example, major depression with melancholic features shares many common features with major depression without melancholic features. Is it reasonable to assume that with such overlap clinicians can reliably distinguish the two? Even if they can is there any value to doing so? This depends on whether we're prepared to assume that the underlying causes or maintenance factors are the same or different. If these disorders are driven by the same underlying mechanism then they should respond to the same treatments. If, however, certain subtypes respond better to certain treatments then there is a value to demarcating the disorders because it ensures better patient care.

A related point is that not only do the subtypes overlap with the major depressive classifications, but they overlap with other disorders too. For example, borderline personality disorder is characterised by a history of self-harm, out-of-control emotions, suicidality, and an oversensitivity to abandonment, and it is also highly associated with anxiety and panic. Depression is characterised by suicidal thoughts, out-of-control emotions, is often associated with self-harm and can include an oversensitivity to abandonment (depression with atypical symptoms). What's more, depression is highly associated with anxiety and panic. What does this tell us about the way in which we classify these disorders? Clearly, there are common themes between depression and borderline personality disorder; although depression isn't associated with the 'clinginess' of borderline personality disorder, many other features are common. So can these disorders be reliably distinguished?

Quick test

1. What is the difference between major depression and bipolar disorder?

2. What are the subtypes of depression and what are their characteristic features?

Does depression come from thinking?

Without question, one of the most influential clinical contributions was Aaron Beck's cognitive model of depression. The ideas from this model have underpinned virtually every cognitive model of every disorder covered in this book (and a great many more besides). This section describes Beck's model and the evidence for it.

CRUCIAL CONCEPT

A **cognitive schema** (at least in Beck's terminology) is simply a belief about something. **Schemata**, the plural, are a set of assumptions or beliefs about things.

Beck's cognitive model

Beck's (1967) model of depression and his subsequent formulation of cognitive therapy (Beck, 1976) hinge on the idea that during early life we develop a set of schemata based on our experience. In depressed people these schemata, or assumptions, develop from negative early experiences such as the loss of a parent, rejection or criticism from friends, parents or teachers, or even the depressed behaviour of a parent. These negative experiences lead to the development of dysfunctional beliefs about the world, which are triggered by critical incidents in the future. So, for example, failing your clinical psychology exam might trigger a set of beliefs such as 'I am stupid', 'people will always hate what I do', 'I am a worthless person'. Once the negative schema is activated this leads to a stream of what Beck called, negative automatic thoughts (NATs).

CRUCIAL CONCEPT

Negative automatic thoughts (NATs) are a set of automatically-evoked thoughts over which the person has no voluntary control (a bit like a stream of intrusive thoughts).

These NATs are interpreted as being true by the individual and are not evaluated and, therefore, lead to other negative thoughts. It is this negative stream of consciousness that leads to the symptoms of depression: the NATs disrupt mood, reduce motivation, increase anxiety/arousal, disrupt cognitive processing especially through misattributions and interpretive biases, and lead to behavioural changes. Figure 7 shows this process.

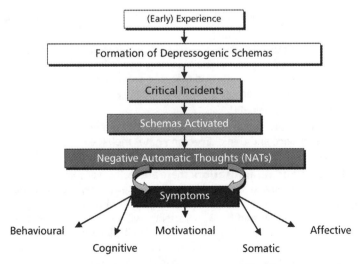

Figure 7: Beck's (1967) cognitive model of depression

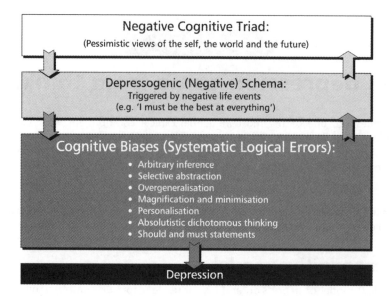

Figure 8: Depressive cognitions

Beck further elaborated on the types of cognitions in depression and the relationship between them (see Figure 8). He argued that negative schema (as just described) maintain the **negative cognitive triad**, which is a set of three far-reaching and global views:

- **Pessimistic views of the self.** These views relate to the person's subjective evaluation of themselves ('I am useless').

- **Pessimistic views of the world.** This refers to the person's subjective feeling of not being able to cope with the demands of the environment ('I cannot cope with the demands placed upon me'). These views do not reflect global world concerns (e.g. the state of the environment), but necessarily involve the person directly ('this job is too much for me to deal with').

- **Pessimistic views of the future.** These are beliefs about the negative state of the future, or that things will not change for the better and again concern subjective events ('I will never be able to do this job properly').

The negative schemas also lead to cognitive biases/distortions. Beck listed a number of possible biases, which he called **systematic logical errors**:

- **Arbitrary inference**: 'my friend didn't answer their doorbell, they must be avoiding me.'

- **Selective abstraction**: despite a wealth of evidence that someone likes you, you pick up on occasional negative signals. So, in a new relationship, the person tells you they'd really like to see you again and that they really like you but that they're busy for a few days. You might interpret their unavailability as a signal of their 'true' feelings: that they don't really like you.

- **Overgeneralisation**: this is global thinking. For example, you have an argument with an acquaintance and think, 'Everyone hates me'. Clearly the argument with this one person does not influence all of your other relationships.

- **Magnification and minimisation**: these are really over-playing potential negative events and under-playing positive ones. So, for example, magnification would be taking a relatively minor incident and blowing it out of proportion (e.g. you're late to meet someone in a pub and think 'my friends will think I'm always late', clearly this sentiment ignores the fact that your friends will place you being late within the context of all of the times you've been punctual). Minimisation would be playing down positive feedback (e.g. someone says that you look really good today and you think that they said that only because you usually look even worse but today you just look slightly less horrendous than normal).

- **Personalisation**: this is the 'world revolving around me' syndrome. It involves attributing random negative events to you despite evidence to the contrary (e.g. believing that it's all your fault that no one is enjoying themselves at a party).

- **Absolutistic dichotomous thinking**: this is basically 'thinking in black and white' or 'all or nothing' thoughts. Examples of this could be 'If I fail my exams, my life is ruined', or 'without my girlfriend, I am nothing'. There is no room to see alternatives.

- **'Should' and 'must' statements**: these are beliefs about what the person should and shouldn't do and generally reflect the schemata that the person has. Examples are 'I must be best at everything' and 'I must be liked by everyone'.

There are numerous clinical reports that depressives do actually think in these ways (for example, Beck, 1976). However, this merely means that Beck's model is a good descriptor of the cognitions that depressives have. It tells us nothing about how these cognitions come about. Like most of the models we've come across in this book they describe the processes but say nothing about the mechanisms behind these processes (why is it that some people acquire these thought processes whereas others don't?).

Quick test

1. What are negative automatic thoughts?
2. What are examples of depressogenic schemas?
3. What is the negative cognitive triad?

Section 3

Can we learn to be depressed?

If people who are depressed have the cognitive biases described above, then it's possible that they learn them. This section looks at the most influential theory of how depression might be learnt: learned helplessness theory. First we'll look at some of the experiments that led to the theory before taking a look at contemporary views of learned helplessness.

Learned helplessness theory

Martin Seligman and his colleagues did several experiments in the 1960s demonstrating how the control of aversive outcomes was linked to helplessness in dogs (Overmier & Seligman, 1967; Seligman & Maier, 1967).

CRUCIAL STUDY

Seligman's basic paradigm used chambers that had two compartments separated by a barrier. Both sides of the chamber were floored with mesh through which a strong electrical current could be passed – thus shocking anything that happened to be in that compartment. They used two groups of dogs. In the first part of the experiment, the first group of dogs could escape the electric shocks by jumping across the barrier to the opposite compartment, in which the shock was not activated – they had control. For the second group, however, both compartments were electrified, so wherever the dogs moved they received a shock – they had no control over negative events. In the second stage of the experiment, both groups of dogs could escape the shock by jumping the barrier and entering the opposite compartment; however, the dogs that had no control in the first part of the experiment didn't do this; instead they cowered passively in a corner and whimpered. In fact, even when the experimenters dragged them across the barrier into the safe chamber, they did not learn that they could escape the shock. Seligman concluded that these dogs had learned to be helpless.

The learned helplessness theory of depression (Seligman, 1975) evolved from these experiments and suggests that depression arises from a perception that important environmental events cannot be controlled. For example, loss of a loved one or repeated abuse may lead to passivity and a belief that these external negative events cannot be controlled. This idea was subsequently extended by Abramson, Seligman and Teasdale (1978) who suggested that humans differed from animals in that they make attributions about events and their consequences. A causal attribution is simply an explanation of why an event happened, and according to Abramson *et al.*, certain people explain negative events by causes that are:

- **internal**: 'it's my fault that I fell out with my friend';
- **stable over time**: 'the reason why I fell out with my friend will happen over and over again';
- **global in effect**: 'I will fall out with other friends.'

Abramson *et al.* suggested that people who make these types of causal attributions are more likely to blame themselves for negative events and to expect to experience negative events in the future. The resulting expectations lead to increased helplessness and loss of self-esteem. These internal, global and stable attributions are not entirely dissimilar to Beck's cognitive triad.

Abramson *et al.* went on to argue that in humans experiences of uncontrollable outcomes are not enough for helplessness to develop. Instead, they must experience an objectively uncontrollable event (like the shocked dogs) but they must also perceive this event and past events as uncontrollable. The crucial factor is the attribution of these negative events as internally caused, stable and global. Such an attribution leads to expectations that future events will be uncontrollable and with this expectation comes a sense of helplessness.

In actual fact, the evidence for this model is less than encouraging. For example, Coyne & Gotlib (1983) in a thorough review of the evidence at the time concluded that there is, at best, only equivocal support for the revised learned helplessness model. Also, this model doesn't say anything about cause and effect: there is no explanation of what causes a pessimistic attributional style, and whether this style develops because of other factors that actually ultimately cause the depression. Also, like Beck's model, there is no attempt to explain manic episodes.

Quick test

What is learned helplessness?

Section 4

What's the role of serotonin in depression?

If Beck's model and Seligman's learned helplessness models can't really explain from where depressive thought styles come, then perhaps biology can. We saw in Chapter 2 that the limbic system is the communication network between the brain-stem and the cortex and involves the hypothalamus (which itself controls basic functions such as eating, drinking and sexual activity and helps us feel pain and pleasure). You might also remember that the limbic system has a crucial role in emotion and that neurons in the limbic system use noradrenergic neurotransmitters for communication: **norepinephrine**, **serotonin** and **dopamine**. If the limbic system is involved in emotion, then it's an obvious candidate to explain depression. This section looks at the role of neurotransmitters in the development of depression, and one neurotransmitter in particular: serotonin.

Monoamine theories

Possibly the most widely held layperson belief about clinical psychology is that depression is caused by a reduction in the levels of serotonin in the brain. Most laypeople may not know that it's specifically in the limbic system, but they do know that serotonin is the cause. Partly this is because of the widespread use of antidepressant medication and the publicity it has attracted. However, the actual biological theory is based on three neurotransmitters known as the monoamine group; they are serotonin, dopamine and norepinephrine. However, it is true to say that much of the research has been based on serotonin and norepinephrine and less is known about the role of dopamine. However, manic episodes are believed to be caused by an increase in the levels of the monoamine neurotransmitters and dopamine especially has been implicated. There are a few ways that these increases or decreases in neurotransmitters could occur (at this point having a quick look back at Chapter 2 might be useful to remind yourself of what the terms mean):

- **Increased degradation**. If there is too much degradation, then too much of the neurotransmitter is absorbed leaving low levels in the synaptic gap (synapses).
- **Impaired release or reuptake**. Low levels of monoamine neurotransmitters could be due to too little of the neurotransmitter being released in the first place, or too much reuptake after the nerve pulse has been transmitted, which would also leave a low level of the neurotransmitter in the synaptic gap.

The monoamine theories actually originate from a lucky accident: a drug called imipramine was being tested as an antipsychotic agent in schizophrenics, and the experimenters noticed that it had an antidepressant effect on these patients. Imipramine is one of a class of drugs now-called **tricyclic antidepressants** (TCAs) and these drugs affect dopermi-nergic receptors and serotonin (5-HT) and norepinephrine (NE) transporters; it is the effect on the latter two that is believed to reduce depression. It has subsequently been found that drugs that block the reuptake of serotonin (**selective serotonin reuptake inhibitors**, or **SSRIs**) such as fluoxetine (Prozac) also reduce depressed symptoms, by blocking the reuptake of serotonin thus leaving more in the synapse (in layman's terms it increases the amount of serotonin available in the limbic system). However, before getting too excited read the section on 'do drug therapies work?'.

Other evidence (Malone & Mann, 1993, McBride *et al.*, 1994) suggests that people with major depressive disorder may have fewer monoamine receptors, or less sensitive receptors than those without depression. The effect of this would be an inefficient use of the neurotransmitter in the synaptic gap (functionally the same as having a low level of these neurotransmitters).

Finally, literally thousands of studies have now been done in which the by-products of neurotransmitters (in blood and urine) are measured in depressed and non-depressed groups. Initial evidence suggested that levels were lower in depressed groups; however, the vast wealth of literature that has now evolved suggests that this is not always the case and consistent differences between depressed and non-depressed groups are not always found (Thase & Howland, 1995). This evidence is difficult to assess because of the difficulty and inaccuracy of methods for measuring these by-products.

Quick test

What is the role of monoamine neurotransmitters in depression?

Section 5

How is depression treated?

All the theories of depression that we've looked at have been biological, or heavily cognitively influenced. It's no great shock then to discover that both cognitive-based therapies and drug therapies are reported to be extremely successful in the treatment of depression (at least at face value). This section overviews these two therapies and assesses their efficacy.

Drug therapy

There are several drug therapies available that act in different ways (see Gumnick & Nemeroff, 2000 for an excellent review):

- **Tricyclic antidepressants (TCA)**. Examples of these are imipramine, amitriptyline (Elavil) and doxepin (Sinequan). These drugs affect doperminergic receptors and serotonin (5-HT) and norepinephrine (NE) transporters. It is the effect on the latter two that is believed to reduce depression.
- **Selective serotonin reuptake inhibitors (SSRI)**. Examples of these include fluoxetine (Prozac), paroxetine (Paxil in the USA and Seroxat in the UK) and sertraline (Zoloft). These drugs block the reuptake of serotonin thus leaving more in the synapse (in layman's terms it increases the amount of serotonin available in the limbic system).
- **Monoamine oxidase inhibitors (MAOI)**. Examples of these drugs are phenelzine (Nardil), isocaboxazid, and tranyleypromine (Parnate). These drugs inhibit monoamine oxidase, an enzyme that destroys both serotonin and neropinephrine, thus it increases the functional level of these two neurotransmitters. These drugs have a permanent effect.
- **Serotonin-norepinephrine reuptake inhibitors (SNRI)**. The newest forms of antidepressants inhibit the reuptake of both serotonin and norepinephrine and are available in the form of the drug venlafaxine (Effexor).

Does drug therapy work?

Common wisdom is now that antidepressants have a substantial effect on depressive symptoms and these drugs are now widely prescribed not only by psychiatrists but also by general practitioners. Most of the available evidence relates to tricyclic antidepressants (often imipramine), although all antidepressants have to go through clinical trials before the Food and Drug Administration (FDA) pass them.

Success rates for TCAs reduce symptoms in about 50–70% of depressed patients (although bear in mind that placebo drugs that have no chemical effect have a positive influence in 20–30% of patients!). However, TCAs have many drawbacks also: they all have side effects (see Gumnick & Nemeroff, 2000 for a review) that pretty much universally include dry mouth, urinary and bowel retention, tachy-cardia, blurred vision and sexual dysfunction.

However there has been a recent backlash: many clinical trials of antidepressant medication have been criticised because of the clinicians knowing which patients were receiving the antidepressants and which were receiving a placebo (see Greenberg, 2001; Greenberg, Bornstein, Zborowski, Fisher, & Greenberg, 1994; Greenberg, Bornstein, Greenberg, & Fisher, 1992; Antonuccio, Danton, DeNelsky, Greenberg, & Gordon, 1999). This leads to biases in favour of the drugs from the drug-favouring therapists. However, Quitkin, Rabkin, Gerald, Davis and Klein (2000), in a review of this literature, concluded that the benefit of antidepressants is, nevertheless, substantiated.

Cognitive therapy for depression

The key feature of cognitive therapy is challenging thoughts and beliefs. This involves behavioural experiments and data collection to disprove the client's interpretations and beliefs about events. A key process is in making clients realise that the thoughts they have are merely thoughts and do not necessarily reflect the true state of affairs. Several standard procedures are used to achieve this:

Thought catching

This involves listing thoughts following some troublesome event. So therapy might begin by focusing on a recent incident that has led to depression and listing the thoughts and feelings that the person had. The therapist and client determine which thoughts are reasonable reflections of reality and which are NATs brought on by the incident.

Task assignment

Tasks are generated (largely by the client) that reflect activities that the client is avoiding for whatever reason (for example, avoiding going out because of fear of rejection). The client then makes predictions about what will go wrong should such a task be acted out. Between sessions the client is encouraged to do the task, and in the subsequent session the client and therapist discuss the extent to which the client's predictions were accurate (usually they will have overestimated the negativity of the task).

Reality testing

This is a similar procedure but is focused on disproving specific beliefs (rather than looking at avoided activities). So tasks are generated to test out the reality of a given belief (for example, phoning a friend to disprove the belief that no one wants to speak to the person).

Cognitive rehearsal

Once tasks have been performed, cognitive rehearsal can be used to help the client develop skills for overcoming problems. If a situation is likely to arise in the near future that is similar to the task they have performed, the client is encouraged to think about every detail of this future event. Whenever they come across a difficulty, it is noted down and set aside so that the client can follow the task through to a happy conclusion (and focus on the positive feelings that this successful completion elicits). The stumbling blocks are then discussed one by one, and the client is encouraged to generate solutions to each one. A particular block can also be dealt with using a task assignment (depending on the nature of the block). This helps clients to practise generating solutions to problems.

Alternative therapy

This technique is primarily to overcome feelings of helplessness and focuses on coping options. The client generates situations about which they feel unable to cope. They are then encouraged to generate a number of alternative solutions or courses of action for a given situation. They are encouraged to generate any option no matter how ridiculous or seemingly counter-productive. The benefits and costs of each alternative are then discussed. These techniques aim to promote lateral thinking and break the cycle of thoughts such as 'I can't do anything to control this.'

Dealing with underlying fears and beliefs

Finally, the therapist seeks to examine the ways in which certain thoughts or avoidance behaviours indicate underlying fears (e.g. fear of rejection) or core beliefs (e.g. 'unless I'm best at something there is no point in me doing it'). The history of how these beliefs developed should be discussed with the therapist and client exchanging ideas about what vulnerability factors exist within the client. These core beliefs should again be challenged using tasks.

Does cognitive therapy work?

There are literally hundreds of studies looking at the effect of CBT (as described above) on depression. Williams (1992) reviews these studies and suggests that CBT alone produces a change in depressed outpatient symptoms of around 66%. Compare this to the values for drug therapy and you can see that there is a similar benefit. CBT is nearly always as good as drugs alone but has none of the side-effects. Drugs are usually as good as CBT but in some studies come out as marginally worse. Combinations of CBT and antidepressants afford little benefit over CBT alone; however, drugs can be useful if depression is severe to stabilise the client enough for CB techniques to be implemented.

Quick test

1. What are the different types of antidepressants and how do they work?

2. What techniques are used in cognitive therapy for depression?

Section 6

End of chapter assessment

Questions

1. What is depression?

2. What are the subtypes of depression? Are they easily distinguished?

3. Does Beck's cognitive model of depression fully explain the disorder?

4. Have depressed people simply learned to be helpless?

5. How do antidepressants work and are they a useful clinical tool?

6. How can depression be treated and how do these treatments work?

Section 7

Further reading

Fennell, M. J. V. (1989). Depression. In K. Hawton, P. M. Salkovskis, J. Kirk, and D. M. Clark (Eds.), *Cognitive Behaviour Therapy for Psychiatric Problems: A Practical Guide* (pp. 169–234). Oxford: Oxford University Press. (A wonderful look at how cognitive behaviour therapy is put into practice.)

Gumnick, J. F., & Nemeroff, C. B. (2000). Problems with currently available antidepressants. *Journal of Clinical Psychiatry*, *61* (supplement 10), 5–15. (This is advanced, but gives a lovely overview of the different antidepressants.)

Williams, J. M. G. (1992). *The Psychological Treatment of Depression: A Guide to the Theory and Practice of Cognitive Behaviour Therapy*. London: Routledge. (Like Fennell above, a really nice overview of theory and practice, but with more detail, Williams writes in a very engaging style also.)

Chapter 9
Schizophrenia

Chapter summary

This chapter looks at schizophrenia by first describing the symptoms associated with the disorder and how these symptoms cluster to form subtypes of the disorder. The role of the family in the development of schizophrenia is then explored by looking at the genetic influences, and then the role of parental personality types and communication styles. We move on to look at biological models and these hinge on three differences between schizophrenics and control patients:

- levels of dopamine appear to be higher in schizophrenics' brains;
- schizophrenics appear to have enlarged ventricles, that result in smaller hippocampal regions; and
- the pathway between the cerebellum, hypothalamus and frontal cortex appears to be dysfunctional in many schizophrenics.

These neuropsychological findings can be integrated into a cognitive framework and we look at two such attempts: Frith's model of schizophrenia and Andreasen's idea that schizophrenia is a disorder of consciousness. Finally, we look at how schizophrenia is still predominantly treated with neuroleptic drugs (phenothiazines) before exploring what role clinical psychology has, beyond drug therapies, for treating this complex and disturbing disorder.

Assessment targets

After reading this chapter you should be able to:

Target 1: Explain the key diagnostic criteria for schizophrenia. Question 1 at the end of this chapter tests you on this.

Target 2: Explain the subtypes of schizophrenia. Question 2 at the end of this chapter tests you on this.

Target 3: Explain the dopamine hypothesis and its implication for treatment. Question 3 at the end of this chapter tests you on this.

Target 4: Explain what structural abnormalities are, and how they explain schizophrenic symptoms. Question 4 at the end of this chapter tests you on this.

Target 5: Describe how communication patterns in families contribute to relapse in schizophrenia. Question 5 at the end of this chapter tests you on this.

Target 6: Describe how schizophrenia is explained in cognitive terms. Question 6 at the end of this chapter tests you on this.

Target 7: Describe how schizophrenia is treated and know whether these treatments are successful. Question 7 at the end of this chapter tests you on this.

Section 1

What is schizophrenia?

Although the layperson typically thinks that schizophrenia is a split personality it is, in fact, a disorder characterised by a diverse and complex set of symptoms and is one of the most debilitating psychiatric disorders. Despite what the media might have us believe, people with schizophrenia are far more likely to be victims of violence and crime than to commit violent acts themselves: people with schizophrenia have an increased risk of violent behaviour only when untreated or when engaging in substance abuse. Schizophrenia has a prevalence of about 1%, and this rate is fairly consistent across countries.

Schizophrenia was first isolated as a pathological condition by Kraepelin (1922) who described it in terms of a set of specific symptoms, which have since been subdivided into positive and negative ones – see below. This section looks at these symptoms, and how schizophrenia is diagnosed.

Symptoms of schizophrenia

The symptoms of schizophrenia are varied, and were originally divided into two categories (Crow, 1980a): **positive symptoms (type 1)** and **negative** ones **(type 2)**. However, more recent work (Lenzenweger, Dworkin & Wethington, 1991) has identified a third sub-class of symptoms known as **disorganisation symptoms**. As we shall see later, these subclasses map onto the three main types of schizophrenia.

Positive symptoms
These symptoms are said to add something to the patient's behaviour. Examples of these are: delusions of grandeur and persecution, in which the patient feels they have the power of life and death over others or that others are out to get them; hallucinations, which are usually auditory and often lead to the misconception that the patient is being controlled by an outside force. Some schizophrenics also believe that their thoughts are being broadcast to other people and the advent of television has led to some related hallucinations (sometimes patients believe that the television is spying on them or that the programmes are actually their thoughts being broadcast into millions of homes).

Negative symptoms
These symptoms take away from the patient's behaviour and take the form of flat affect, lack of initiative and persistence, social withdrawal and an inability to experience pleasure (Crow, 1980a). These symptoms typically manifest themselves in withdrawal. The content of speech can deteriorate (they talk a lot but 'say' very little) and they can have poverty of speech (they don't say very much at all), they can be unmotivated, lack interest and energy (**avolition** or **apathy**), they can become incapable of experiencing pleasure (**anhedonia**), and become **asocial** (have few friends and find social interaction difficult).

Disorganisation
These symptoms relate to disorganised or bizarre behaviours and actions.

Unclassified symptoms
These three categories of symptoms are all well and good, but there are other common symptoms that don't fit comfortably into these categories and are known as **unclassified symptoms**.

Catatonia: patients may gesture repeatedly (using peculiar and sometimes complex sequences of finger, hand and arm movements); have seemingly excessive energy and manic behaviour; they may adopt strange postures for large amounts of time (**catatonic immobility**); they sometimes show what's called **waxy flexibility** (in which their limbs can be positioned by another person and the patient will maintain that position for long periods of time).

Inappropriate affect: it is also common for schizophrenics to display inappropriate emotions (such as laughing at bad news).

CRUCIAL CASE STUDIES

To get a feel for the diversity of symptoms found in schizophrenia, here are some examples of the types of delusions and hallucinations that schizophrenics experience (taken from Davison & Neale, 2000, who themselves drew upon Mellor, 1970).

Delusions
Bodily sensations imposed from external agents: 'X-rays entering the back of my neck, where the skin tingles and feels warm, they pass down the back in a hot tingling strip about six inches wide to the waist.' (male, 29)

Thoughts are not their own: 'I look out of the window and I think the garden looks nice and the grass looks cool, but the thoughts of Eamon Andrews come into my mind. There are no other thoughts there, only his... He treats my mind like a screen and flashes his thoughts on it like you flash a picture.' (female, 29)

Their thoughts are being broadcast: 'As I think, my thoughts leave my head on a type of mental ticker-tape. Everyone around has only to pass the tape through their mind and they know my thoughts.' (female, 21)

Hallucinations
Hearing voices (commentating, or arguing): 'The 32-year-old housewife complained of a man's voice speaking in an intense whisper from a point about two feet above her head. The voice would repeat almost all of the patient's goal-directed thinking – even the most banal thoughts. The patient would think, 'I must put the kettle on,' and after a pause of not more than one second the voice would say, 'I must put the kettle on.' It would often say the opposite: 'Don't put the kettle on.'

Inappropriate effect
Laughing at bad news: 'Mama's sick. (Giggle.) Sicky, sicky, sicky. (Giggle.) I flipped off a doctor once, did you know that? Flip. I want to wear my blue dress tomorrow. Dress mess (giggle)'. (Female, when asked about her recently hospitalised mother.)

Diagnosing schizophrenia

Now we know a little about the symptoms in schizophrenia we can look at how *DSM-IV* actually diagnoses the disorder.

CRUCIAL DIAGNOSIS

DSM—IV characterises schizophrenia as follows:

A. **Characteristic symptoms.** Two (or more) of the following, each present for a significant portion of time during a one-month period (or less if successfully treated):

- delusions;
- hallucinations;
- disorganised speech (e.g., frequent derailment or incoherence);
- grossly disorganised or catatonic behaviour;
- negative symptoms (e.g., affective flattening, alogia, or avolition).

Note: Only one criterion A symptom is required if delusions are bizarre or hallucinations consist of a voice keeping up a running commentary on the person's behaviour or thoughts, or two or more voices conversing with each other.

B. **Social/occupational dysfunction**. For a significant portion of the time since the onset of the disturbance, one or more major areas of functioning such as work, interpersonal relations, or self-care are markedly below the level achieved prior to the onset (or when the onset is in childhood or adolescence, failure to achieve expected level of interpersonal, academic or occupational achievement).

C. **Duration**. Continuous signs of the disturbance persist for at least six months. This six-month period must include at least one month of symptoms (or less if successfully treated) that meet criterion A (i.e. active-phase symptoms) and may include periods of prodromal or residual symptoms. During these prodromal or residual periods, the signs of the disturbance may be manifested by only negative symptoms or two or more symptoms listed in criterion A present in an attenuated form (e.g. odd beliefs, unusual perceptual experiences).

D. **Schizoaffective and mood disorder exclusion**. **Schizoaffective disorder** and **mood disorder with psychotic features** have been ruled out because either (i) no major depressive, manic, or mixed episodes have occurred concurrently with the active-phase symptoms; or (ii) if mood episodes have occurred during active-phase symptoms, their total duration has been brief relative to the duration of the active and residual periods.

E. **Substance/general medical condition exclusion**. The disturbance is not due to the direct physiological effects of a substance (e.g. a drug of abuse, a medication) or a general medical condition.

F. **Relationship to a pervasive developmental disorder**. If there is a history of **autistic disorder** or another **pervasive developmental disorder**, the additional diagnosis of schizophrenia is made only if prominent delusions or hallucinations are also present for at least a month (or less if successfully treated).

There are five subtypes of schizophrenia that are recognised in *DSM-IV* also:

Paranoid schizophrenia. A type of schizophrenia in which the following criteria are met:

- preoccupation with one or more delusions or frequent auditory hallucinations, and
- none of the following is prominent: disorganised speech, disorganised or catatonic behaviour, or flat or inappropriate affect.

Catatonic schizophrenia. A type of schizophrenia in which the clinical picture is dominated by at least two of the following:

- motoric immobility as evidenced by catalepsy (including waxy flexibility) or stupor;
- excessive motor activity (that is apparently purposeless and not influenced by external stimuli);
- extreme negativism (an apparently motiveless resistance to all instructions or maintenance of a rigid posture against attempts to be moved) or mutism;
- peculiarities of voluntary movement as evidenced by posturing (voluntary assumption of inappropriate or bizarre postures), stereotyped movements, prominent mannerisms, or prominent grimacing;
- echolalia (repetitive imitation of other people's speech) or echopraxia (repetition imitation of other people's movements). This is the sort of behaviour seen in the film *Awakenings* that was based on Sacks' (1991) book.

Disorganised schizophrenia. A type of schizophrenia in which all of the following are prominent: disorganised speech, disorganised behaviour, and flat or inappropriate affect. The criteria for catatonic type must not be met.

Undifferentiated schizophrenia. A type of schizophrenia in which symptoms that meet criterion A are present, but the criteria are not met for the paranoid, disorganised, or catatonic type.

Residual schizophrenia. A type of schizophrenia characterised by the absence of prominent delusions, hallucinations, disorganised speech, and grossly disorganised or catatonic behaviour. There is continuing evidence of the disturbance, as indicated by the presence of negative symptoms or two or more symptoms listed in criterion A for schizophrenia, present in an attenuated form (e.g. odd beliefs, unusual perceptual experiences).

Quick test

1. What are the differences between hallucinations and delusions?

2. What are the subtypes of schizophrenia?

3. How do positive symptoms differ from negative symptoms of schizophrenia?

Section 2

Do our families make us schizophrenic?

Schizophrenia is one disorder that has very strong genetic foundations. However, the family also seems to play a role in sometimes creating a social environment conducive to the disorder developing. This section first looks at genetic influences on schizophrenia before moving on to social theories.

Genetic influences on schizophrenia

There is strong evidence for a genetic component of schizophrenia with Gottesman, McGuffin & Farmer (1987) finding that 44.30% of monozygotic twins (from the same egg) both have schizophrenia compared to only 12.08% of dizygotic twins (twins from different eggs). In addition, in siblings, around 7.30% will both have schizophrenia, 9.35% of children with a schizophrenic parent will develop the disorder, and 2.84% of children with a schizophrenic grandparent will develop the disorder.

However, because the actual incidence rate in monozygotic twins – who are genetically identical – is below 100% there is evidence that this genetic factor may only increase an individual's susceptibility to the disorder. One possibility is that the genes provide deficiencies in the brain that cause cognitive impairments (see the next section), but that environmental factors are needed to trigger the actual symptoms.

Social influences on schizophrenia

The first clue that family factors might have a role to play in schizophrenia came from Fromm-Reichmann (1948) who suggested that certain mothering styles lead to schizophrenia. The '**schizophrenogenic mother**' was characterised as a cold, dominant, and conflict-inducing mother who would reject her children yet be over-protective, be insensitive to others' feelings, have rigid and moralistic views of sex and fear intimacy. Subsequent research did not support the link between this parenting style and schizophrenia; nevertheless Fromm-Reichmann was not too far from some important contributing factors. Bateson, Jackson, Haley, & Weakland (1956) produced a similar theory to the schizophrenogenic mother: they suggested that parents (mothers in particular) of children who develop schizophrenia put their children in '**double binds**' (i.e. they send their children conflicting messages). For example, a child having fallen from a swing, a mother might on the one hand act overprotectively and offer physical comfort whilst shouting at the child for being so careless. Again, little subsequent empirical support for this idea has emerged.

CRUCIAL CONCEPTS

Communication deviance refers to unclear, unintelligible, or oddly worded communication during family transactions. It's the inability of a speaker to share the focus of attention with a listener when delivering a spoken message (Singer & Wynne, 1966).

Expressed emotion is the tendency of a relative to criticise, be hostile or demonstrate emotional over-involvement (Miklowitz & Goldstein, 1993).

More recent theories revolve around communication deficiencies such as communication deviance and expressed emotion. The basic idea is that this communication deviance inhibits the child from learning to develop logical thought, and to perceive or process incoming information. These vulnerabilities manifest in the core symptoms of schizophrenia.

Communcation deviance

Communication deviance (CD) is typically measured in one of two ways. **Thematic Apperception Tests (TAT-CD)** involve showing patients several ambiguous pictures and asking them to invent a story around the picture. The story generated is supposed to reflect the person's way of perceiving things. These stories are coded to reflect two broad categories:

- disorders of linguistic-verbal reasoning (unclear sentences, fragmented ideas etc.); and
- disorders of perceptual-cognitive processing (inability to construct a story around the elements in the picture, or distorting the images in some way).

The second measure is **Interactional Communication Deviance (ICD)**, which involves an unstructured problem-focused family interaction task that is then coded much the same as the TAT–CD. Levels of communication deviance are typically higher in parents of schizophrenics than among parents of non-psychotic or normal individuals (Miklowitz & Stackman, 1992). Communication deviance also seems to predict future mental illness: Goldstein (1987) found that 28% of 64 disturbed but not psychotic patients had developed broad-spectrum schizophrenic symptoms some 15 years after their parents' communication styles were assessed. However, this study tells us little about whether these effects are specific to schizophrenia, or whether other disorders would respond in a similar way to communication deviance. Also, these patients began the study disturbed, and so this shows only that communication deviance worsens the disturbance, and doesn't necessarily cause it.

Expressed emotion

Expressed emotion (EE) is a categorical construct: you are either high on EE or low on EE with no underlying continuum assumed. Again, there are two main measures. The **Camberwell Family Interview (CFI**, Vaughn & Leff, 1976) involves a 60–90 minute semi-structured interview of key relatives (usually parents) conducted just as the patient is hospitalised and explores the relatives' emotional reaction to the developing psychosis. One of three emotional attitudes must be expressed for someone to be classified as high expressed emotion; these are high hostility, high criticism and over-involvement. This method is linked to a current psychotic episode, is long and cumbersome to administer and does not incorporate the patient's attitude towards the parent. Therefore the **Five Minute Speech Sample (FMSS**, Magana *et al.*, 1986) was developed in which a five-minute speech sample of a relative talking about what kind of person the patient is and how the two of them get along is recorded. Apparently, this five-minute segment can be quickly coded to reveal high or low EE. However, although the classification of low EE seems fairly reliable (80–93% concordance with an average of 89%), the classification of high EE is much more variable (40–100% concordance and an average of 60%) – see Miklowitz & Goldstein, 1993.

High scores on expressed emotion have been linked to relapse in schizophrenia (Koenigsberg & Handley, 1986) with an average relapse rate of 51.2% in high EE families and only 22% in low EE families.

Quick test

1. Is there a genetic influence on schizophrenia?

2. What are expressed emotion and communication deviance and how do they contribute to schizophrenia?

Section 3

The role of the brain in schizophrenia

If social factors can't fully explain the development of schizophrenia then perhaps the genetic connection that we've seen manifests itself in dysfunctional brain chemistry or structures. This section explores this possibility by looking first at the role of neurotransmitters, then at structural abnormalities in schizophrenic brains.

The dopamine hypothesis

By far the greatest treatment breakthrough for schizophrenia was the accidental discovery by Delay & Deniker and Harl (1952) that chlorpromazine had a dramatic effect on schizophrenic symptoms. Chlorpromazine is a neuroleptic drug (one of the family called phenothiazines) that acts like dopamine molecules, thus preventing the 'real' molecules from firing synapses (i.e. they inhibit the natural dopamine in the brain). These drugs inhibit the positive symptoms of schizophrenia (see Section 1 in this chapter to remind yourself of the distinction between positive and negative symptoms). In addition, amphetamines (which block the reuptake of dopamine and hence increase levels in the synapse) and L-DOPA (which increases the synthesis of dopamine) both cause the positive symptoms of schizophrenia to occur and cause the recognised disorder of 'amphetamine psychosis', which can outlast the effects of the drug. So there is evidence that the reduction of dopamine levels reduces the positive symptoms whilst increases in dopamine levels bring on the symptoms. This evidence led to 'the dopamine hypothesis': schizophrenia is the result of increased levels of dopamine in the brain.

Although this tells a nice story, there are several problems with this theory. First, the drugs do not affect the negative symptoms at all. Second, phenothiazines act on dopamine levels within a day and yet symptoms do not disappear for several days or weeks after the drugs are taken. Therefore, something must be taking place between the interval when the dopamine is blocked and the symptoms are relieved. Third, dopamine is widely implicated in Parkinson's disease (and other motor disorders), which means that we don't have a clear mechanism by which to translate elevated levels of dopamine into the behavioural symptoms of schizophrenia (because dopamine is also associated with different behaviours). However, we can rescue the dopamine hypothesis from this last criticism thanks to the work of Crow (1980b) who found two main pathways in the brain in which dopamine is distributed: the **substantia nigra–caudate putamen** pathway and the **ventral tegmental area (VTA)–nucleus accumbens septi (NAS)** pathway. The NAS is part of the basal ganglia in the limbic system. Crow demonstrated that the effectiveness of different phenothiazines drugs on schizophrenic symptoms is correlated with the degree to which those drugs bind with receptors for dopamine in the NAS but not with the degree to which they bind with receptors in the caudate putamen. This is just as well because blocking the dopamine in the caudate putamen would induce Parkinson's disease in the schizophrenics. One of the challenges of the pharmaceutical companies has been to develop drugs that maximise the effect on schizophrenic symptoms whilst minimising the symptoms of Parkinson's disease.

Big holes in the brain?

There is good evidence that schizophrenic patients do have structural abnormalities in their brain. We saw in Chapter 2 the brain is full of fluid-filled holes called ventricles. If the ventricles are particularly large, then they are taking up space that would otherwise be occupied with brain tissue. According to work from the mid-1980s (e.g. Brown *et al.*, 1986; see Tyrer & MacKay, 1986 for a review), if you look carefully at the brains of dead schizophrenics you see very consistent signs of enlargement in the part of the lateral ventricle in the temporal lobe. You can demonstrate similar losses in living schizophrenics using brain scanning. These quantitative studies on the temporal lobe of schizophrenics implies that there is an enlargement of this ventricle and this in turn implies that there has been a loss of cortical tissue in the temporal lobes.

CRUCIAL CONCEPTS

Computed axial tomography (CT or CAT scan). A beam of X-rays passes horizontally through the brain and then moves progressively through 360 degrees. A plate opposite the source of the X-ray measures the radioactivity that passes through the brain. From this, a computer can construct a two-dimensional image of a 'slice' of a patient's brain.

Magnetic resonance imaging (MRI). The patient's body is placed in a huge magnetic field, which causes the hydrogen atoms in the body to move. When the magnet is switched off the atoms return to their original positions producing a small electromagnetic signal. A computer uses these signals to construct images of the brain tissue. These images are vastly superior to those produced by CT scans.

Functional Magnetic Resonance imaging (fMRI) does much the same thing but takes the pictures so quickly that it can detect changes in the brain's metabolic rate, thus, areas of the brain that are 'working' light up in the images!

Weinberger, Torrey, Neophytides, & Wyatt (1979) compared computed tomography (CT) scans of 73 chronic schizophrenics and observed lateral ventricles nearly twice as large as 56 control subjects. However, this evidence is fairly non-specific because ventricles may increase in size to compensate for tissue loss almost anywhere in the brain. Weinberger, Berman, and Zec (1986) investigated **regional cerebral blood flow (rCBF)** in patients and controls whilst performing the **Wisconsin Card Sort Test (WCST)**, a reliable indicator of functioning in a particular area of the frontal lobe, the dorsolateral prefrontal cortex (DLPFC). They took measurements on the task as subjects inhaled air containing radioactive xenon. The results were comparable except that schizophrenics did not show increased blood flow to the DLPFC during a number matching test, unlike controls. This adds weight to the argument favouring frontal lobe pathology in schizophrenia. Brown *et al.* (1986) conducted a study comparing 41 schizophrenic patients with 29 patients with affective disorder and found that schizophrenic brains were 6% lighter and had enlarged lateral ventricles (19% larger in the anterior horn and 97% larger in the temporal horn) compared to those of affective psychosis patients. Roberts (1990) asserts that the expansion of these lateral ventricles in schizophrenics is primarily at the expense of tissue in the hippocampus and parahippocampal gyrus (PHG). Roberts argues alterations in the functional capabilities of the PHG may have impact on connecting areas such as the frontal lobe (e.g. the DLPFC mentioned above).

More recent studies suggest that the loss of tissue in the brains of schizophrenics may be more extreme than was first thought: Bachneff (1991) reviewed the evidence from MRI studies and suggests that they reveal quite widespread losses of cortical tissue, and Bornstein, Schwarzkopf, Olson, and Nasrallah, (1992) have shown that there is a correlation between the degree of cognitive impairment in schizophrenics and the size of the third ventricle (this ventricle lies in the middle of the thalamus).

Evidence about enlarged ventricles should be treated cautiously because it is unclear whether ventricle enlargement is a direct consequence of schizophrenia leading to cortical cell loss or vice versa. Nevertheless the suggestion of the involvement of the temporal lobe in schizophrenia is very attractive because the temporal lobe structures are considered important for both cognitive functions (like memory) and as a link between the cognitive systems of the brain and the systems responsible for emotional reactions. Schizophrenia involves both cognitive an emotional disturbances.

Connections in the brain

Andreasen (1997) and her colleagues have attempted to localise the various symptoms of schizophrenia in brain regions through the use of fMRI techniques. They found consistent abnormalities in frontal, thalamic and cerebellar regions in schizophrenic patients. Andreasen postulated that the symptoms of schizophrenia arise from impaired connectivity between these regions and suggested that schizophrenics have a dysfunction of cognitive measurement (she called this **cognitive dysmetria**). Essentially, this means that a person with schizophrenia cannot take measure of time and space or make inferences about interrelationships between the self and others, or among past, present and future. So schizophrenics cannot coordinate the perception, prioritisation, retrieval and expression of experiences and ideas.

This hypothesis has received strong support from Andreasen and her colleagues who have found abnormalities in the frontal-thalamic-cerebellar circuitry of schizophrenics across a broad range of cognitive tasks.

Quick test

1. Describe the dopamine hypothesis.
2. What is the effect of enlarged ventricles?
3. What brain pathway is implicated in schizophrenia?

Section 4

Cognitive theories of schizophrenia

We've seen that most of the symptoms of schizophrenia involve cognitive distortions. We've also looked at how brain dysfunctions might lead to these dysfunctions. However, we haven't looked at whether these dysfunctions can be placed within the context of a coherent cognitive model. This section briefly outlines Frith's cognitive model of schizophrenia, which attempts to integrate some of the neurological evidence into a cognitive framework. We end the section by looking at how these concepts can be reconciled with neuropsychological perspectives on schizophrenia.

Cognitive theories (Frith, 1992)

Frith has divided the symptoms of schizophrenia into three broad groups or dimensions:

- **disorders of willed action** (which lead to symptoms such as alogia and avolition);
- **disorders of self-monitoring** (which lead to symptoms such as auditory hallucinations and delusions of alien control);
- **disorders in monitoring the intentions of others** ('mentalising') (which lead to symptoms such as 'formal thought disorder' and delusions of persecution).

Frith believes that these are all special cases of a more general underlying mechanism: a disorder of consciousness or self-awareness that impairs the ability to think with metarepresentations (Frith, 1992). So, in essence, schizophrenics are unable to represent their own or others' mental states, which leads them to misinterpret their thoughts as being external and to interpret others' intentions as hostile. In short, they lack a fundamental ability to 'hold constant' many of the things that normal people do in everyday interactions (for example, they cannot make the usual assumptions that another person's intent is benign). .

CRUCIAL CONCEPT

A **metarepresentation** is a higher order representation of mental states. In other words, it is a representation of what you or others are thinking or intending to do.

The evidence so far for Frith's model comes from two lines of research (see Andreasen, 1997, for a review).

Willed action

This is tested by giving people tasks for which the correct response is not evident from the context. A frontal circuit is activated in normal people during such tasks; however schizophrenic patients show relative decreases in these frontal regions and increases in temporal regions compared with controls (Frith, Friston, Liddle & Frackowiak, 1991; Liddle et al., 1992). If the verbal fluency task is slowed down, however, frontal function in the schizophrenics becomes like that of controls but the temporal abnormality remains (Frith, 1995). If you examine the relationship between blood flow in frontal and temporal regions you find that the normal relationship between them has broken down in schizophrenics (McGuire & Frith, 1996).

Hallucinations

Frith and colleagues suggest that hallucinations are due to schizophrenics erroneously attributing their own inner speech to another person. This reflects a defect in self-monitoring. They developed a task aimed at mimicking hallucinations: people performed a sentence completion task but imagined that the responses were spoken by another person. McGuire and Frith (1996) found that this task led to activation of speech production and perception regions in the brain (the areas activated were Broca's area, the supplementary motor area, and the left superior and middle temporal regions). They used the same task on a group of schizophrenics (and with this group compared those with hallucinations against those without); hallucinators had decreased flow in brain areas used to monitor speech (such as the left middle temporal gyrus and supplementary motor area).

Integrative models

Andreasen (1997) noted the common threads between different conceptual approaches to schizophrenia: in all these theories schizophrenia reflects a disruption in a fundamental cognitive process that affects specific circuitry in the brain. The terminology and concepts differ – Frith talks about metarepresentations and Andreasen speaks in terms of cognitive dysmetria – but both convey a common theme: the cognitive dysfunction in schizophrenia is inefficient temporal and spatial referencing of information and experience as the person attempts to determine boundaries between the self and not-self and to formulate effective decisions or plans that will guide him or her through the small-scale (speaking a sentence) or large-scale (finding a job) manoeuvres of daily living. Andreasen suggests that this capacity is what we might call 'consciousness'. So, in short, Andreasen suggests that schizophrenia is a disorder of consciousness.

Quick test

1. Explain Frith's model of schizophrenia.

2. Explain Andreasen's model of schizophrenia.

Section 5

How is schizophrenia treated?

We've had a look at various theories of schizophrenia. The final part of this chapter examines how these theories are put into practice in therapeutic settings. In reality, most schizophrenics are treated with drugs (see section on the dopamine hypothesis). However, as more has become known about the contributions that families make to relapse, family therapy has become a useful treatment tool in recent years. Finally, very recent developments have been made with using cognitive therapy to treat some schizophrenic symptoms. This section briefly explores each of these in turn.

Drug therapy

Schizophrenia is mainly treated with medication (neuroleptic drugs), which is unsurprising given the biological slant of nearly all of the theories. Phenothiazines (chlorpromazine) and their variants, which reduce the functional level of dopamine in the brain, are still used today and are effective on about 70% of patients. They seem like a great success story in that they relieve a great many patients of the most disturbing symptoms and allow them to lead relatively normal lives. On the down side, 30% of patients don't respond at all, and these drugs do not address the negative symptoms (which makes you wonder whether these symptoms are actually part of the same disorder!). They also have side effects. I mentioned earlier on that neuroleptics could bring on Parkinson-like symptoms (known as extrapyramidal symptoms). These are things like body tremor and rigidity (think of the boxer Mohammed Ali, who suffers from Parkinson's disease), restless leg syndrome and muscular contraction. Tardive dyskinesia is also common (abnormal movements especially of the face and tongue) especially after drug withdrawal. There are several other effects such as sedation, weight gain, and in females the absence of menstruation and excessive lactation. Reynolds (1992) does an excellent review of the various drugs and their effects and side effects.

Cognitive behaviour therapy

CBT aims to change some of the maladaptive behaviours that are associated with the schizophrenia. Hall (1989) has indicated the use of token economies in shaping appropriate behaviour and this technique can be applied to the negative symptoms of schizophrenia. What's more, the patient will have spent a long time trying to explain the sensory overloads that they have experienced. If these experiences are suddenly removed through drugs it will be necessary to rehabilitate the patient to reality. CBT also aims to challenge the dysfunctional assumptions that patients have acquired about their experiences. CBT is used in addition to drug therapies (not instead of) to improve coping skills (to deal with symptoms), to provide problem-solving training, and to reduce relapse by challenging delusions and thought stopping (see Haddock *et al.*, 1998 for a review). Recent evidence suggests that this helps to reduce the positive symptoms above and beyond drug therapy (Tarrier *et al.*, 1998).

─────────── CRUCIAL CONCEPT ───────────

A token economy is a system (usually in an inpatient setting) in which 'good' or 'appropriate' behaviour is rewarded with tokens that can be exchanged for desirable luxuries. It works on basic learning principles: behaviours that the therapist wants to encourage are rewarded, and so are more likely to happen again.

Family therapy

In recent years therapies have been developed that aim to modify the disruptive communication patterns found in families containing a schizophrenic. **Behavioural**

family management (BFM) is one such attempt to modify expressed emotion and communication deviance. This therapy has three major components:

- educating the family about schizophrenia (this helps to remove attributions of blame from the patients);
- communications skills training in which parents and patients are shown their negative communications patterns and are helped to change them by learning basic conversational skills; and
- problem-solving skills in which both parties are taught how to approach problem situations in a collaborative way.

This therapy takes place over a nine-month period with around 21 sessions.

Other family programmes have emphasised the need for family meetings at home and actively engaging the family member in discussions on how best to cope with specific problems in family life. Typically, therapists work with the family to resolve any difficulties and to generate a wide variety of ideas and how they should be implemented. Families should also be encouraged to express their feelings very clearly and explicitly. Strachan (1988) has systematically reviewed four studies and concluded that subjects under these therapies show less social withdrawal and lower rates of relapse. Relatives also display more positive attitudes as well.

However, these programmes cannot be used on individuals who have eroded their family's tolerance or who choose a solitary life. Whilst the biological approaches and therapeutic interventions are very different in their nature they have complementary roles to play. They are not opposing forces but integrate to form a unified whole. Whilst drugs can offer some relief to most of the positive symptoms they have little effect on the negative ones. Conversely, therapy can do little about the positive symptoms but seems quite effective at facilitating integration back into family life and society in general.

How successful is therapy?

We've seen that neuroleptic drugs are effective for about 70% of patients. In terms of family therapy, Falloon *et al.* (1985) studied 36 relatively chronic schizophrenics after nine months of BFM. They found that BFM with medication reduced relapse rates more than medication and individual therapy. As such, family therapy seems to help in reducing relapse rates. It also had a positive effect in the dose of neuroleptic medication needed and social adjustment. The same study revealed evidence that the communication and problem-solving training was effective in reducing parent EE. Therapy also reduced communication deviance overall, however inspection of the data suggested that this was due to reductions in the patients more than their parents. However, it is noteworthy that these dimensions improve from neuroleptic medication alone.

Quick test

1. What drugs are effective for schizophrenia?
2. How is family therapy used in the treatment of schizophrenia?

THE LEARNING CENTRE
TOWER HAMLETS COLLEGE
ARBOUR SQUARE
LONDON E1 0PS

Section 6

End of chapter assessment

Questions

1. What are the key symptoms of schizophrenia?

2. What are the subtypes of schizophrenia?

3. What is the dopamine hypothesis and what is its implication for treatments of schizophrenia?

4. Is schizophrenia caused by 'big holes in the brain'?

5. What role do families play in the development of schizophrenia?

6. How do cognitive models attempt to explain schizophrenia?

7. How can schizophrenia be treated and are these treatments effective?

Section 7

Further reading

Andreasen, N. C. (1997). Linking mind and brain in the study of mental illness: a project for a scientific psychopathology. *Science*, *275*, 1586-93. (Excellent, but high level, summary of recent neurological evidence.)

Miklowitz, D. J., & Goldstein, M. J. (1993). Mapping the intrafamilial environment of the schizophrenic patient. In R. L. Cromwell and C. R. Snyder (Eds.) *Schizophrenia: Origins, Processes, Treatments and Outcome*. New York: Oxford University Press. (Excellent overview of family factors in schizophrenia.)

References

Abramson, L. Y., Seligman, M. E. P., & Teasdale, J. (1978). Learned helplessness in humans: critique and reformulation. *Joural of Abnormal Psychology*, *87*, 49–74.

Aitken, R. C. B., Lister, J. A., & Main, C. J. (1981). Identification of features associated with flying phobias in aircrew. *British Journal of Psychiatry*, *139*, 38–42.

Akhtar, S., Wig, N. N., Varma, V. K., Pershad, D., & Verma, S. K. (1975). A phenomenological analysis of symptoms in obsessive-compulsive neurosis. *British Journal of Psychiatry*, *127*, 342–348.

American Psychiatric Association (1952). *Diagnostic and Statistical Manual of Mental Disorders*. Washington, DC: Author.

American Psychiatric Association (1968). *Diagnostic and Statistical Manual of Mental Disorders* (2nd ed.). Washington, DC: Author.

American Psychiatric Association (1987). *Diagnostic and Statistical Manual of Mental Disorders* (3rd ed. revised). Washington, DC: Author.

American Psychiatric Association (1980). *Diagnostic and Statistical Manual of Mental Disorders* (3rd ed.). Washington, DC: Author.

American Psychiatric Association (1994). *Diagnostic and Statistical Manual of Mental Disorders* (4th ed.). Washington, DC: Author.

American Psychological Association (APA) (1993). *Task Force on Promotion and Dissemination of Psychological Procedures. A Report to the Division 12 Board of the American Psychological Association.* (Available from Division 12 of the American Psychological Association, 750 First Street, NE, Washintgon, DC 20002–4242, USA.)

Andreasen, N. C. (1997). Linking mind and brain in the study of mental illness: a project for a scientific psychopathology. *Science*, *275*, 1586–1593.

Antonuccio, D. O., Danton, W.G., DeNelsky, G. Y., Greenberg, R. P., Gordon, J. S. (1999). Raising questions about antidepressants. *Psychotherapy and Psychosomatics*, *68*, 3–14.

Apter, J. T. & Allen, L. A. (1999). Buspirone: future directions. *Journal of Clinical Psychopharmocology*, *19*, 86–93.

Bachneff, S. A. (1991). Positron emission tomography and magnetic resonance imaging: a review and a local circuit neurons hypo(dys)function hypothesis of schizophrenia. *Biological Psychiatry*, *30*, 857–886.

Ball, S. G., Otto, M. W., Pollack, M. W. & Rosenbaum, J. F. (1994). Predicting prospective episodes of depression in patients with panic disorder: a longitudinal study. *Journal of Consulting and Clinical Psychology*, *62,* 359–365.

Ballenger, J. C., Burrow, G. D., Dupont, R. L, Lesser, I. M., Noyes, R., Pecknold, J. C., Rifkin, A. & Swinson, R. P. (1988). Alprazolam in panic disorder and agoraphobia: results from a multicenter trial. I. efficicacy in short-term treatment. *Archives of General Psychiatry*, *45*, 413–422.

Bateson, G., Jackson, D. D., Haley, J., & Weakland, J. (1956). Toward a theory of schizophrenia. *Behavioural Science*, *1*, 251–264.

Bauer, D. H. (1976). An exploratory study of developmental changes in children's fears. *Journal of Child Psychology and Psychiatry*, *17*, 69–74.

Baxter, L. R., Schwartz, J. M., Guze, B. H., Bergman, K., & Szuba, M.P. (1990). PET imaging in obsessive-compulsive disorder with and without depression. *Journal of Clinical Psychiatry*, *51*, 61–69 suppl.

Beck, A. T. (1967). *Depression: Clinical, Experimental and Theoretical Aspects*. New York: Harper & Row.

Beck, A. T. (1976). *Cognitive therapy and the emotional disorders*. New York: International Universities Press.

Beck, A. T., Emery, G., & Greenberg, R. L. (1985). *Anxiety Disorders and Phobias: A Cognitive Perspective*. New York: Basic Books.

Beck, A. T., Ward, C. H., Mandelson, M., Moch, J. E., & Erlbaugh, J. (1962). Reliability of psychiatric diagnosis: II. A study of consistency of clinical judgements and ratings. *American Journal of Psychiatry, 119*, 351–357.

Borkovec, T. D. (1994). The nature, functions and origins of worry. In G. C. L. Davey & F. Tallis (Eds.), *Worrying: Perspectives on Theory, Assessment and Treatment* (pp. 5–33). Chichester: Wiley.

Borkovec, T. D., & Costello, E. (1993). Efficacy of applied relation and cognitive-behavioural therapy in the treatment of generalized anxiety disorder. *Journal of Consulting and Clinical Psychology, 61*, 611–619.

Borkovec, T. D., & Inz, J. (1990). The nature of worry in generalized anxiety disorder: a predominance of thought activity. *Behaviour Research and Therapy, 28*, 153–158.

Bornstein, R. A., Schwarzkopf, S. B., Olson, S. C., & Nasrallah, H. A. (1992). Third-ventricle enlargement and neuropsychological deficit in schizophrenia. *Biological psychiatry, 31*, 954–961.

Bouton, M. E., Mineka, S., Barlow, D. H. (2001). A modern learning theory perspective on the etiology of panic disorder. *Psychological Bulletin, 108*, 4–32.

Brown, R., Colter, N., Corsellis, J. A. N., Crow, T. J., Frith, C. D., Jagoe, R., Johnstone, E. C. (1986). Postmortem evidence of structural brain changes in schizophrenia: differences in brain weight, temporal horn area, and parahippocampal gyrus compared with affective disorders. *Archives of General Psychiatry, 43*, 36–42.

Bruch, H. (1973). *Eating Disorders: Obesity, Anorexia Nervosa and the Person Within*. New York: Basic Books.

Butler, G. (1985). Exposure as a treatment of social phobia: some instructive difficulties. *Behaviour Research and Therapy, 23*, 651–657.

Butler, G. (1989). Phobic disorders. In K. Hawton, P.M. Salkovskis, J. Kirk and D.M. Clark (Eds.), *Cognitive Behaviour Therapy for Psychiatric Problems: A Practical Guide* (pp. 97–128). Oxford: Oxford University Press.

Butler, G., Fennell, M., Robson, P., & Gelder, M. (1991). Comparison of behaviour therapy and cognitive behaviour therapy in the treatment of generalized anxiety disorder. *Journal of Consulting and Clinical Psychology, 59*, 167–175.

Campbell, S. B. (1986). Developmental issues in childhood anxiety. In R. Gittelman (Ed.), *Anxiety Disorders of Childhood*, (pp. 24–57). New York: Guilford.

Caplan, P. J. & Gans, M. (1991). Is there empirical justification for the category of self-defeating personality disorder? *Feminism and Psychology, 1*, 263–278.

Channon, S., de Silva, P., Hemsley, D., & Perkins, R. (1989). A controlled trial of cognitive-behavioural and behavioural treatment of anorexia nervosa. *Behaviour Research and Therapy, 27*, 529–535.

Clark, D. A. (1986). A cognitive approach to panic. *Behaviour Research and Therapy, 24*, 461–470.

Clark, D. A., & Purdon, C. L. (1995). The assessment of unwanted intrusive thoughts: a review and critique of the literature. *Behaviour Research and Therapy, 33*, 967-976.

Clark, D. A., Salkovskis, P. M., Hackmann, A., Middleton, H., Anastasiades, P., & Gelder, M. G. (1994). A comparison of cognitive therapy, applied relaxation and imipramine in the treatment of panic disorder. *British Journal of Psychiatry, 164*, 759–769.

Clark, D. M. & Fairburn, C. G. (1997). *Science and Practice of Cognitive Behaviour Therapy*. Oxford: Oxford University Press.

Clark, D. M. & Wells, A. (1995) A cognitive model of social phobia. In R. Heimberg, M. Liebowitz, D. A. Hope & F. R. Schneier (Eds.) *Social Phobia: Diagnosis, Assessment and Treatment*. New York: Guilford Press.

Cooper, P. J., & Fairburn, C. G. (1992). Thoughts about eating, weight and shape in anorexia nervosa and bulimia nervosa. *Behaviour Research and Therapy, 30*, 501–511.

Cooper, P. J., & Fairburn, C. G. (1993). Confusion over the core psychopathology of bulimia nervosa. *International Journal of Eating Disorders, 13*, 385–389.

Coyne, J. C., & Gotlib, I. H. (1983). The role of cognition in depression: a critical appraisal. *Psychological Bulletin, 94*, 472–505.

Craighead, L. W., & Agras, W. S. (1991). Mechanisms of action in cognitive behavioural and pharmacological interventions for obesity and bulimia nervosa. *Journal of Consulting and Clinical Psychology, 59*, 115–125.

Craske, M. G., Rapee, R. M., Jackel, L., & Barlow, D. M. (1989). Qualitative dimensions of worry in *DSM-III-R* generalised anxiety disorder subjects and non-anxious controls. *Behaviour Research and Therapy, 27*, 397–402.

Crow, T. J. (1980a). Molecular pathology of schizophrenia: more than one disease process? *British Medical Journal, 280*, 66–68.

Crow, T. J. (1980b). Positive and negative schizophrenic symptoms – the role of dopamine. *British Journal of Psychiatry, 137*, 383–386.

Davey, G. C. L. (1994). The 'disgusting' spider: the role of disease and illness in the perpetuation of fear of spiders. *Society and Animals, 3*, 17–24.

Davey, G. C. L. (1995). Rumination and the enhancement of fear: some laboratory findings. *Behavioural and Cognitive Psychotherapy, 23*, 203–215.

Davey, G. C. L. (1997). A conditioning model of phobias. In G. C. L. Davey (Ed.) *Phobias: A Handbook of Theory, Research and Treatment* (pp. 301–322). Chichester: Wiley.

Davey, G. C. L., de Jong, P. J., & Tallis, F. (1993). UCS inflation in the aetiology of a variety of anxiety disorders: some case histories. *Behaviour Research and Therapy, 31*, 495–498.

Davey, G. C. L. & Field, A. P. (in press). Learning and Conditioning. In McGhee, P. (Ed.), *Introduction to Contemporary Psychology*. London: Palgrave.

Davey, G. C. L., Field, A. P., & Startup, H. M. (in press). Repetitive and iterative thinking in psychopathology: anxiety-inducing consequences and a mood-as-input mechanism. In R. Menzies, & P. De Silva (Eds.), *Obsessive Compulsive Disorders: Theory, Research and Treatment*. Chichester: Wiley.

Davey G. C. L., & Levy, S. (1998). Catastrophic worrying: personal inadequacy and a perseverative iterative style as features of the catastrophising process. *Journal of Abnormal Psychology, 107*, 576–586.

Davey, G. C. L., & Tallis, F. (Eds.) (1994). *Worrying: Perspectives on Theory, Assessment and Treatment*. Chichester: Wiley.

Davison, G. C., & Neale, J. M. (2000). *Abnormal Psychology* (8th edition). New York: Wiley.

Delay, J., Deniker, P., & Harl, J.-M. (1952). Traitement des états d'excitation et d'agitation par une méthode médicamenteuse dérivé de l'hibernothérapie. *Annuls Médecine Psychologie, 110*, 262–267.

Dollinger, S. J., O'Donnell, J. P. & Staley, A. A. (1984). Lightning-strike disaster: effects on children's fears and worries. *Journal of Consulting and Clinical Psychology, 52* (6), 1028–1038.

Dritschel, B. H., Williams, K., & Cooper, P. J. (1991). Cognitive distortions against women experiencing bulimic episodes. *International Journal of Eating Disorders, 10*, 547–555.

Durham, R. C., Murphy, T., Allan, T., Richard, K., Treliving, L. R., & Fenton, G. W. (1994). Cognitive therapy, analytic psychotherapy and anxiety management training for generalized anxiety disorder. *British Journal of Psychiatry, 165*, 315–323.

Ekman, P., & Friesen, W. V. (1971). Constants across cultures in the face and emotion. *Journal of Personality and Social Psychology, 17*, 124–129.

Enard, W., Khaitovich, P., Klose, J., Zöllner, S., Heissig, F., Giavalisco, P., Nieselt-Struwe, K., Muchmore, E., Varki, A., Ravid, R., Doxiadis, G. M., Bontrop, R. E., & Pääbo, S. (2002). Intra- and interspecific variation in primate gene expression patterns, *Science, 296*, 340–343.

Eysenck, H. J. (1952). The effects of psychotherapy: an evaluation. *Journal of Consulting Psychology, 16*, 319–324.

Eysenck, H. J. (1985). *Decline and Fall of the Freudian Empire*. London: Penguin.

Eysenck, M. W., Mogg, K., May, J., Richards, A. & Mathews, A. (1991). Bias in interpretation of ambiguous sentences related to threat in anxiety. *Journal of Abnormal Psychology, 100,* 144–150.

Fairburn, C. G. (1997). Eating disorders. In D. M. Clark and C. G. Fairburn (Eds.), *Science and Practice of Cognitive Behaviour Therapy* (pp. 209–241). Oxford: Oxford University Press.

Fairburn, C. G., Shafran, R. & Cooper, Z. (1999) A cognitive behavioural theory of anorexia nervosa. *Behaviour Research and Therapy, 37,* 1–13.

Fairburn, C. G., Norman, P. A., Welch, S. L., O'Connor, M. E., Doll, H. A., & Peveler, R. C. (1995). A prospective study of outcome in bulimia nervosa and the long-term effects of three psychological treatments. *Archives of General Psychiatry, 52,* 304–312.

Falloon, I. R. H., Boyd, J. L., McGill, C. W., Williamson, M., Razani, J., Moss, H. B., Gilderman, A. M., Simpson, G. M. (1985). Family management in the prevention of morbidity of schizophrenia: clinical outcome of a 2-year longitudinal study. *Archives of General Psychiatry, 42,* 887–896.

Fals-Stewart, W., Marks, A. P., & Schafer, J. (1993). A comparison of behavioural group therapy and individual behaviour therapy in treating obsessive-compulsive disorder. *Journal of Nervous and Mental Disease, 181,* 189–193.

Fava, M., Copeland, P. M., Schweiger, U., & Herzog, D. B. (1989). Neurochemical abnormalities of anorexia nervosa and bulimia nervosa. *American Journal of Psychiatry, 146,* 963–971.

Fehm, L. & Margraf, J. (2002). Thought suppression: specificity in agoraphobia versus broad impairment in social phobia? *Behaviour Research and Therapy, 40,* 57–66.

Ferguson, C. P., La Via, M. C., Crossan, P. J., Kaye, W. H. (1999). Are serotonin selective reuptake inhibitors effective in underweight anorexia nervosa? *International Journal of Eating Disorders, 25,* 11–17.

Field, A. P. (in press). *Discovering Abnormal and Clinical Psychology.* London: Sage.

Field, A. P., Argyris, N. G., & Knowles, K. A. (2001). Who's afraid of the big bad wolf?: a prospective paradigm to test Rachman's indirect pathways in children. *Behaviour Research and Therapy, 39,* 1259–1276.

Field, A. P. & Davey, G. C. L. (2001). Conditioning models of childhood anxiety. In W. K. Silverman, & P. A. Treffers (Eds.) *Anxiety Disorders in Children and Adolescents: Research, Assessment and Intervention* (pp. 187–211). Cambridge: Cambridge University Press.

Field, A. P., & Hole, G. (2002). *How to Design and Report Experiments.* London: Sage.

Field, A. P., & Lawson, J. (2002). Fear information and the development of fears during childhood: effects on implicit fear responses and behavioural avoidance. Manuscript submitted for publication.

Foa, E. B., Amir, N., Bogert, K. V. A., Molnar, C., & Przeworski, A. (2001). Inflated perception of responsibility for harm in obsessive-compulsive disorder. *Journal of Anxiety Disorders, 15,* 259–275.

Foa, E. B., & Kozak, M. (1993). Obsessive-compulsuive disorder: long-term outcome of psychological treatment. In M. Mavissakalian, & R. Prien (Eds.), *Long-term Treatment of Anxiety Disorders.* Washington, DC: American Psychiatric Press.

Freud, S. (1954). *The Interpretation of Dreams.* London: George Allen & Unwin Ltd.

Frith, C. D. (1992). *The Cognitive Neuropsychology of Schizophrenia.* Hove: Erlbaum.

Frith, C. (1995). Functional imaging and cognitive abnormalities. *Lancet, 346,* 615–620.

Frith, C. D., Friston, K., Liddle, P. F., & Frackowiak, R. S. J. (1991). Willed action and the prefrontal cortex in man: a study with PET. *Proceedings of the Royal Society of London Series B–Biological Sciences, 244,* 241–246.

Fromm-Reichman, F. (1948). Notes on the development of treatment of schizophrenics by psychoanalytic psychotherapy. *Psychiatry, 11,* 263–273.

Garfinkel, P. E., Kennedy, S. H., & Kaplan, A. S. (1995). Views on classification and diagnosis of eating disorders. *Canadian Journal of Psychiatry, 40,* 445–456.

Gelder, M. G., Bancroft, J. H. J., Gath, D. H., Johnston, D. W., Mathews, A. M., & Shaw, P. M. (1973). Specific and non-specific factors in behaviour therapy. *British Journal of Psychiatry, 123,* 445–462.

Goldstein, A. J. & Chambless, D. L. (1978) A re-analysis for agoraphobia. *Behavior Therapy, 9,* 47–59.

Goldstein, M. J. (1987). Family interaction patterns that antedate the onset of schizophrenia and related disorders: a further analysis of data from a longitudinal prospective study. In K. Hahlweg & M. J. Goldstein (Eds.), *Understanding Major Mental Disorder: The Contribution of Family Interaction Research* (pp. 11–32). New York: Family Process Press.

Gorman, J. M., Liebowitz, M. R., Fyer, A. J., Fyer, M. R., Klein, D. F. (1986). Possible respiratory abnormalities in panic disorder. *Psychopharmacology Bulletin, 22,* 797–801.

Gottesman, I. I., McGuffin, P., & Farmer, A. E. (1987). Clinical genetics as clues to the 'real' genetics of schizophrenia. *Schizophrenia Bulletin, 13,* 23–47.

Greenberg, R. P. (2001). Qualms about balms: Perspectives on antidepressants. *Journal of Nervous and Mental Disease, 189,* 296–298.

Greenberg, R. P., Bornstein, R. F., Greenberg, M. D., & Fisher, S., & (1992). A meta-analysis of antidepressant outcome under blinder conditions. *Journal of Consulting and Clinical Psychology, 60,* 664–669.

Greenberg, R. P., Bornstein, R. F., Zborowski, M. J., Fisher, S., & Greenberg, M. D. (1994). A meta-analysis of Fluoxetine outcome in the treatment of depression. *Journal of Nervous and Mental Disease, 182,* 547–551.

Gumnick, J. F., & Nemeroff, C. B. (2000). Problems with currently available antidepressants. *Journal of Clinical Psychiatry, 61* (supplement 10), 5–15.

Hackmann, A., Clark, D. M. & McManus, F. (2000). Recurrent images and early memories in social phobia. *Behaviour Research and Therapy, 37,* 601–610.

Haddock, G., Tarrier, N., Spaulding, W., Yusupoff, L., Kinney, C., & McCarthy, E., (1998). Individual cognitive behaviour therapy in the treatment of hallucinations and delusions: a review. *Clinical Psychology Review, 18,* 821–838.

Hall, J. (1989). Chronic psychiatric handicaps. In K. Hawton, P. M. Salkovskis, J. Kirk and D. M. Clark (Eds.), *Cognitive Behaviour Therapy for Psychiatric Problems: A Practical Guide* (pp. 315–338). Oxford: Oxford University Press.

Heimberg, R. G., Dodge, C. S., Hope, D. A., Kennedy, C. R. & Zollo, L. J. (1990). Cognitive behavioural group treatment for social phobia: comparison with a credible placebo group. *Cognitive Research and Therapy, 14,* 1–23.

Hoebel, B. G., & Tietelbaum, P. (1966). Weight regulation in normal and hypothalamic hyperphagic rats. *Journal of Comparative and Physiological Psychology, 61,* 189–193.

Hofmann, S. G. (2000). Self-focused attention before and after treatment of social phobia, *Behaviour Research and Therapy, 38,* 717–725.

Holland, A. J., Hall, A., Murray, R., Russell, G. F. M., & Crisp, A. H. (1984). Anorexia nervosa: a study of 34 twin pairs and one set of triplets. *British Journal of Psychiatry, 145,* 414–419.

Jansen, A. (2001). Towards effective treatment of eating disorders: nothing is as practical as a good theory. *Behaviour Research and Therapy, 39,* 1007–1022.

Jenike, M. A. (1993a). Augmentation strategies for treatment-resistant obsessive-compulsive disorder. *Harvard Review of Psychiatry, 1,* 17–26.

Jenike, M. A. (1993b). Obsessive-compulsive disorder: efficacy of specific treatments as assessed by controlled trials. *Psychopharmacology Bulletin, 29,* 487–499.

Jimerson, D. C., Lesem, M. D., Kaye, W. H., Hegg, A. P., & Brewerton, T. D. (1990). Eating disorders and depression: is there a serotonin connection? *Biological Psychiatry, 28,* 443–454.

Jimerson, D. C., Wolfe, B. E., Metzger, E. D., Finkelstein, D. M., Cooper, T. B. & Levine, J. M. (1997). Decreased serotonin function in bulimia nervosa. *Archives of General Psychiatry, 54,* 529–534.

Jones, M. K., & Menzies, R. G. (1998). The relevance of associative learning pathways in the development of obsessive-compulsive washing. *Behaviour Research and Therapy, 36,* 273–283.

Kalucy, R. S., Crisp, A. H., & Harding, B. (1977). A study of 56 families with anorexia nervosa. *British Journal of Medical Psychology, 50*, 381–395.

Karno, M., & Golding, J. M. (1991). Obsessive compulsive disorder. In L. R. Robins & D. A. Regier (Eds.), *Psychiatric Disorders in America: The Epidemiologic Catchment Area Study*. New York: Maxwell Macmillan International.

Kaye, W. H., Greeno, C. G., Moss, H., Fernstrom, J., Fernstrom, M., *et al.* (1998). Alterations in serotonin activity and psychiatric symptoms after recovery from bulimia nervosa. *Archives of General Psychiatry, 55*, 927–935.

Kaye, W. H., Gwirtsman, H. E., George, D. T., & Ebert, M. H. (1991). Altered serotonin activity in anorexia nervosa after long-term weight restoration: does elevated cerebrospinal-fluid 5-hydroxyindoleacetic acid level correlate with rigid and obsessive behaviour? *Archives of General Psychiatry, 48*, 556–562.

Kazdin, A. E. & Wilcoxin, L. A. (1976). Systematic desensitisation and non-specific treatment effects: a methodological evaluation. *Psychological Bulletin, 83*, 729–758.

Kendler, K. S. (1975). *The Role of Diagnosis in Psychiatry.* Oxford: Blackwell.

Kendler, K. S., MacLean, C., Neale, M. C., & Kessler, R. C. (1991). The genetic epidemiology of bulimia nervosa. *American Journal of Psychiatry, 148*, 1627–1637.

Kendler, K. S., Neale, M. C., Kessler, R. C., & Heath, A. C. (1992). Major depression and generalized anxiety disorder: same genes, (partly) different environments? *Archives of General Psychiatry, 49*, 716–722.

Kennedy, S. H., & Garfinkel, P. E. (1992). Advances in the diagnosis and treatment of of anorexia nervosa and bulimia nervosa. *Canadian Journal of Psychiatry, 37*, 309–315.

Kent, J. & Jambunathan, P. (1989). A longitudinal study of the intrusiveness of cognitions in test anxiety. *Behaviour Research and Therapy, 27*, 43–50.

King, N. H., Gullone, E., & Tonge, B. J. (1993). Self-reports of panic attacks and manifest anxiety in adolescents. *Behaviour Research and Therapy, 31*, 111–116.

Kindt, M., & Brosschot, J. F. (1997). Phobia-related cognitive bias for pictorial and linguistic stimuli. *Journal of Abnormal Psychology, 106*, 644–648.

Kirk, S. A., & Kutchins, H. (1992). *The Selling of DSM: The Rhetoric of Science in Psychiatry.* New York: A. de Gruyter.

Klein, D. E. (1964). Delineation of two drug-responsive anxiety syndromes. *Psychopharmacologia, 5*, 397–408.

Klein, D. F. (1993). Suffocation false alarm theory of panic. *Biological Psychology, 35*, 258–258.

Koenigsberg, H. W., & Handley, R. (1986). Expressed emotion: from predictive index to clinical construct. *American Journal of Psychiatry, 143*, 1361–1373.

Kraepelin, E. (1922). *Manic-depressive Insanity and Paranoia.* Edinburgh: E & S Livingstone.

Krueger, R. F., Caspi, A., Moffitt, T. E., & Silva, P. A. (1998). The structure and stability of common mental disorders (*DSM-III-R*): A longitudinal-epidemiological study. *Journal of Abnormal Psychology, 107*, 216–227.

Langlois, F., Freeston, M. H., Ladouceur, R. (2000). Differences and similarities between obsessive intrusive thoughts and worry in a non-clinical population: study 1. *Behaviour Research and Therapy, 38*, 157–173.

Lascelles, K. R. R., Field, A. P., & Davey, G. C. L. (in press). Using food CSs and body shapes as UCSs: a putative role for associative learning in the development of eating disorders. *Behavior Therapy.*

Lautch, H. (1971). Dental phobia. *British Journal of Psychiatry, 119*, 151–158.

Legg, C. R. (1989). *Issues in Psychobiology.* London: Routledge.

Lemma, A. (1996). *Introduction to Psychopathology.* London: Sage.

Lenzenwenger, M. F., Dworkin, R H., & Wethington, E. (1991). Examining the underlying structure of schizophrenic phenomenology: evidence for a 3-process model. *Schizophrenia Bulletin, 17*, 515–524.

Leonard, K. N., Telch, M. J., & Harrington, P. J. (1999). Dissociation in the laboratory: a comparison of strategies. *Behaviour Research and Therapy, 37*, 49–61.

Levine M.P., Smolak L., Moodey A.F., Shuman M.D. & Hessen L.D. (1994) Normative developmental challenges and dieting and eating disturbances in middle school girls. *International Journal of Eating Disorders, 15,* 11–20.

Lewinsohn, P. M., Zinbarg, R., Seeley, J. R., Lewinsohn, M., & Sack, W. H. (1997). Lifetime comorbidity among anxiety disorders and between anxiety disorders and other mental disorders in adolescents. *Journal of Anxiety Disorders, 11,* 377–394.

Liddle, P. F., Friston, K. J., Frith, C. D., Hirsch, S. R., Jones, T., Frackowiak, R. S. J. (1992). Patterns of cerebral blood-flow in schizophrenia. *British Journal of Psychiatry, 160,* 179–186.

Lunner K., Werthem E.H., Thompson J.K., Paxton S.J., McDonald F. & Halvaarson K.S. (2000) A cross-cultural examination of weight-related teasing, body image, and eating disturbance in Swedish and Australian samples. *International Journal of Eating Disorders, 28,* 430–435.

Lydiard, R. B., Brawman-Mintzer, O. & Ballenger, J. C. (1996). Recent developments in the psychopharmacology of anxiety disorders. *Journal of Consulting and Clinical Psychology, 64,* 660–668.

MacLeod, A. K. (1994). Worry and explanation-based pessimism. In G. C. L. Davey & F. Tallis (Eds.), *Worrying: Perspectives on Theory, Assessment and Treatment* (pp. 115–134). Chichester: Wiley.

Magana, A. B., Goldstein, M. J., Karno, M., Miklowitz, D. J., Jenkins, J., & Falloon, I. R. H. (1986). A brief method for assessing expressed emotion in relatives of psychiatric patients. *Psychiatry Research, 17,* 203–212.

Malone, K., & Mann, J. J. (1993). Serotonin and major depression. In J. J. Mann & D. J. Kupfer (Eds.), *Biology of Depressive Disorders: Part A. A Systems Perspective* (pp. 29–49). New York: Plenum.

Marks, I. M. (1987). *Fears, Phobias and Rituals.* Oxford: Oxford University Press.

Martin, L. L., & Tesser, A. (1989). Toward a motivational and structural theory of ruminative thought. In J. S. Uleman & J. A. Bargh (Eds.), *Unintended Thought* (pp.306-326). New York: Guilford.

Mathews, A. & MacLeod, C. (1994). Cognitive approaches to emotion and emotional disorders. *Annual Review of Psychology, 45,* 25–50.

Mathews, A., Mogg, K., Kentish, J., & Eysenck, M. (1995). Effect of psychological treatment on cognitive bias in generalized anxiety disorder, *Behaviour Research and Therapy, 33,* 293–303.

Mattick, R. P., & Peters, L. (1988). Treatment of severe social phobia: effects of guided exposure with and without cognitive restructuring. *Journal of Consulting and Clinical Psychology, 56,* 251–260.

McBride, P., Brown, R. P., DeMeo, M., & Keilp, J. (1994). The relationship of platelet 5-HT-sub-2 receptor indices to major depressive disorder, personality traits, and suicidal behaviour. *Biological Psychiatry, 35,* 295–308.

McGuire, P. K., & Frith, C. D. (1996). Disordered functional connectivity in schizophrenia. *Psychological Medicine, 26,* 663–667.

McNally, R. J. (1990). Psychological approaches to panic disorder. *Psychological Bulletin, 108,* 403–419.

Mellor, C. S. (1970). First rank symptoms of schizophrenia. *British Journal of Psychiatry, 117,* 15–23.

Menzies, R. G., & Clarke, J. C. (1993a). The etiology of fear of heights and its relationship to severity and individual response patterns. *Behaviour Research and Therapy, 31,* 355–366.

Menzies, R. G., & Clarke, J. C. (1993b). The etiology of childhood water phobia. *Behaviour Research and Therapy, 31,* 499–501.

Miklowitz, D. J., & Goldstein, M. J. (1993). Mapping the intrafamilial environment of the schizophrenic patient. In R. L. Cromwell and C. R. Snyder (Eds.) *Schizophrenia: Origins, Processes, Treatments and Outcome.* New York: Oxford University Press.

Miklowitz, D. J., & Stackman, D. (1992). Communication deviance in families of schizophrenic and other psychiatric patients: current state of the construct. *Progress in Experimental Personality and Psychopathology Research, 15,* 1–46.

Miles, J. (2001). *Research Methods and Statistics.* Exeter: Crucial.

Mineka, S., Davidson, M., Cook, M., & Weir, R. (1984). Observational conditioning of snake fears in rhesus monkeys. *Journal of Abnormal Psychology, 93,* 355–372.

Mitchell, J. E., & deZwaan, M. (1993). Pharmacological treatments of binge eating. In C. E. Fairburn & G. T. Wilson (Eds.), *Binge Eating: Nature, Assessment, and Treatment* (pp. 250–269). New York: Guilford.

Mogg, K., Bradley, B. P., Williams, R., & Mathews, A. (1993). Subliminal processing of emotional information in anxiety and depression. *Journal of Abnormal Psychology, 102,* 304–311.

Mowrer, O. H. (1960). *Learning Theory and Behaviour.* New York: Wiley.

Muris, P., Merckelbach, H., & Collaris, R. (1997). Common childhood fears and their origins. *Behaviour Research and Therapy, 35* (10), 929–937.

Muris, P., Merckelbach, H., Meesters, C., & Van Lier, P. (1997). What do children fear most often? *Journal of Behaviour Therapy and Experimental Psychiatry, 28,* 263–267.

Muris, P., Steerneman, P., Merckelbach, H., & Meesters, C. (1996). Parental modelling and fearfulness in middle childhood. *Behaviour Research and Therapy, 34,* 265–268.

Öhman, A. & Soares, J. J. F. (1994). Unconscious anxiety: phobic responses to masked stimuli. *Journal of Abnormal Psychology, 103,* 231–240.

Ollendick, T. H. & King, N. J. (1991). Origins of childhood fears: an evaluation of Rachman's theory of fear acquisition. *Behaviour Research and Therapy, 29,* 117–123.

Öst, L.-G. (1987). Age of onset in different phobias. *Journal of Abnormal Psychology, 96,* 223–229.

Overmier, J. B., & Seligman, M. E. (1967). Effects of inescapable shock upon subsequent escape and avoidance responding. *Journal of Comparative and Physiological Psychology, 63,* 28–33.

Palmer, J. L. (1988). *Anorexia Nervosa.* London: Penguin.

Polivy J. & Herman C.P. (2002) Causes of eating disorders. *Annual Review of Psychology, 53,* 187–213.

Poulton, R. & Menzies, R. G. (2002). Non-associative fear acquisition: a review of the evidence from retrospective and longitudinal research. *Behaviour Research and Therapy, 40,* 127–149.

Purdon, C. L. (1999). Thought suppression and psychopathology. *Behaviour Research and Therapy, 37,* 1029–1054.

Quitkin, F. M., Rabkin, J. G., Gerald, J., Davis, J. M., and Klein, D. F. (2000). Validity of clinical trials of antidepressants. *American Journal of Psychiatry, 157* (3), 327–337.

Rachman, S. (1977). The conditioning theory of fear acquisition: a critical examination. *Behaviour Research and Therapy, 15,* 375–387.

Rachman, S. (1991). Neoconditioning and the classical theory of fear acquisition. *Clinical Psychology Review, 17,* 47–67.

Rachman, S. (1997). A cognitive theory of obsessions. *Behaviour Research and Therapy, 35,* 793–802.

Rachman, S. J. (1997). The evolution of cognitive behaviour therapy. In D. M. Clark and C. G. Fairburn (Eds.), *Science and Practice of Cognitive Behaviour Therapy* (pp. 3–26). Oxford: Oxford University Press.

Rachman, S. & de Silva, P. (1978). Abnormal and normal obsessions. *Behaviour Research and Therapy, 16,* 233–248.

Rachman, S., Gruter-Andrew, J. & Shafran, R. (2000). Post-event processing in social anxiety. *Behaviour Research and Therapy, 38,* 611–617.

Rachman, S., & Wilson, G. T. (1980). *The Effects of Psychological Therapy.* London: Pergamon.

Rapee, R. M. (1991). Generalized anxiety disorder: A review of clinical features and theoretical concepts. *Clinical Psychology Review, 11,* 419–440.

Rapee, R. M., Brown, T. A., Antony, M. M., Barlow, D. H. (1992). Response to hyperventilation and inhalation of 5.5-percent carbon dioxide-enriched air across the DSM–III–R anxiety disorders. *Journal of Abnormal Psychology, 101*, 538–552.

Rapoport, J. (1989). *The Boy Who Couldn't Stop Washing*. New York: E. P. Dutton.

Reiman, E. M., Raichle, M. E., Robins, E., Butler, F. K., Herscovitch, P., Fox, P., Perlmutter, J. (1986). The application of positron emission tomography to the study of panic disorder. *American Journal of Psychiatry, 143*, 469–477.

Reynolds, G. P. (1992). Developments in the drug treatment of schizophrenia. *Trends in Pharmacological Sciences, 13*, 116–121.

Roberts, G. W. (1990). Schizophrenia: the cellular biology of a functional psychosis. *Trends in Neurosciences, 13*, 207–211.

Roper, G. & Rachman, S. (1976). Obsessional-compulsive checking: experimental replication and development. *Behaviour Research and Therapy, 14*, 25–32.

Rosenhan, D. L. (1973). On being sane in insane places. *Science, 179*, 250–258.

Roth, D., Antony, M. M., & Swinson, R. P. (2001). Interpretations for anxiety symptoms in social phobia. *Behaviour Research and Therapy, 39*, 129–138.

Russell, G. F. M. (1992) Anorexia nervosa of early onset and its impact on puberty. In P. J. Cooper & A. Stein (Eds.) *Feeding Problems and Eating Disorders in Children and Adolescents*. New York: Harwood.

Sacks, O. (1991). *Awakenings* (revised edition). London: Picador.

Salkovskis, P. M. (1999). Understanding and treating obsessive-compulsive disorder. *Behaviour Research and Therapy, 37* (July supplement), S29–S52.

Salkovskis, P. M., Forrester, E. & Richards, C. (1998). Cognitive-behavioural approach to understanding obsessional thinking. *British Journal of Psychiatry, 173*, 53–63 Suppl.

Schwarz, N., & Bless, H. (1991). Happy and mindless, but sad and smart? The impact of affective states on analytic reasoning. In J. Forgas (Ed.) *Emotion and Social Judgements* (pp. 55-71). Oxford: Pergamon.

Seligman, M. E. P. (1971). Phobias and preparedness. *Behavior Therapy, 2*, 307–320.

Seligman, M. E. P. (1975). *Helplessness: On Depression, Development and Death.* San Francisco: Freeman, Cooper.

Seligman, M. E., & Maier, S. F. (1967). Failure to escape traumatic shock. *Journal of Experimental Psychology, 74*, 1–9.

Silverman, W. K. & Nelles, W. B. (1989). An examination of the stability of mothers' ratings of child fearfulness. *Journal of Anxiety Disorders, 3*, 1–5.

Simons, R. C., & Hughes, C. C. (Eds.) (1985). *The Culture-Bound Syndromes: Folk Illnesses of Psychiatric and Anthropological Interest*. Dordrecht: D. Reidel Publishing Company.

Singer, M., & Wynne, L. (1966). Principles for scoring communication deviances in parents of schizophrenics: Rorschach and TAT scoring manuals. *Psychiatry, 29*, 260–288.

Slade, P. D. (1982). Towards a functional analysis of anorexia nervosa and bulimia nervosa. *British Journal of Clinical Psychology, 21*, 167–179.

Smith, M. L., Glass, G. V., & Miller, T. I. (1980). *The Benefits of Psychotherapy*. Baltimore: John Hopkins University Press.

Spitzer, R. L., Williams, J. B. W., & Skodol, A. E. (1980). *DSM–III*: The major achievements and an overview. *American Journal of Psychiatry, 137*, 151–164.

Startup, H. M., & Davey, G. C. L. (2001). Mood-as-input and catastrophic worrying. *Journal of Abnormal Psychology, 110*, 83–96.

Stern, I. & Marks, I. M. (1973). Brief and prolonged flooding. *Archives of General Psychiatry, 28*, 270–276.

Stice, E. (1998). Modelling of eating pathology and social reinforcement of the thin-ideal predict onset of bulimic symptoms. *Behaviour Research and Therapy, 36*, 931-944.

Strachan, A. M. (1988). Family approaches to schizophrenia: recent developments. In F. N. Watts (Ed.) *New Developments in Clinical Psychology Volume 2*. Chichester: Wiley.

Strober, M., Lampert, C., Morrell, W., Burroughs, J., & Jacobs, C. (1990). A controlled family study of anorexia nervosa: evidence of family aggregation and lack of shared transmission with affective disorders. *International Journal of Eating Disorders, 9*, 239–253.

Szasz, T. S. (1971). The sane slave: an historical note on the use of medical diagnosis as justificatory rhetoric. *American Journal of Psychotherapy*, *25*, 228–239.

Tarrier, N., Yusupoff, L., Kinney, C., McCarthy, E., Gledhill, A., Haddock, G., & Morris, J. (1998). Randomised controlled trial of intensive cognitive behaviour therapy for patients with chronic schizophrenia. *British Medical Journal*, *317*, 303–307.

Thase, M. E., & Howland, R. H. (1995). Biological processes in depression: an updated review and integration. In E. E. Beckham & W. R. Leber (Eds.), *Handbook of Depression* (2nd edition, pp. 213–279). New York: Guilford Press.

Turner, S. M., Beidel, D. C., & Stanley, M. A. (1992). Are obsessional thoughts and worry different cognitive phenomena? *Clinical Psychology Review*, *12*, 257–270.

Tyrer, P., & Mackay, A. (1986). Schizophrenia: no longer a functional psychosis. *Trends in Neuroscience*, *9*, 537–538.

Vandereycken, W., Kog, E., & Vanderlinden, J. (1989). *The Family Approach to Eating Disorders*. New York: PMA Publishing Corporation.

Vaughn, C. E., & Leff, J. P. (1976). The influence of family and social factors on the course of psychiatric illness: a comparison of schizophrenic and depressed neurotic patients. *British Journal of Psychiatry*, *129*, 125–137.

Vitousek, K., & Manke, F. (1994). Personality variables and disorders in anorexia nervosa and bulimia nervosa. *Journal of Abnormal Psychology*, *103*, 137–147.

Walsh, B. T., & Devlin, M. J. (1998). Eating disorders: progress and problems. *Science*, *280*, 1387–1390.

Warren, R. & Thomas, J. C. (2001). Cognitive-behavior therapy of obsessive-compulsive disorder in private practice: An effectiveness study. *Journal of Anxiety Disorders*, *15*, 277–285.

Warren, R. & Zgourides, G. D. (1991). *Anxiety Disorders: a Rational-Emotive Perspective*. New York: Pergamon Press.

Watkins, E., & Baracaia, S. B. (2001). Why do people in dysphoric moods ruminate? *Personality and Individual Differences*, *30*, 723–734.

Watson, J.B. & Rayner, R. (1920). Conditioned emotional reactions. *Journal of Experimental Psychology*, *3*, 1–14.

Weinberger, D. R., Berman, K. F., & Zec, R. F. (1986). Physiologic dysfunction of dorsolateral prefrontal cortex in schizophrenia. I. Regional cerebral blood flow evidence. *Archives of General Psychiatry*, *43*, 114–124.

Weinberger, D. R., Torrey, E. F., Neophytides, A. N., & Wyatt, R. J. (1979). Lateral cerebral ventricular enlargement in chronic schizophrenia. *Archives of General Psychiatry*, *36*, 735–739.

Wells, A. (1995). Meta-cognition and worry: a cognitive model of generalised anxiety disorder. *Behavioural and Cognitive Psychotherapy*, *23*, 301–320.

Wells, A., & Butler, G. (1997). Generalized anxiety disorder. In D. M. Clark and C. G. Fairburn (eds.), *Science and Practice of Cognitive Behaviour Therapy* (pp. 155–178). Oxford: Oxford University Press.

Wells, A., Clark, D. M., Salkovskis, P., Ludgate, J., Hackmann, A., & Gleder, M. G. (1995). Social Phobia: the role of in-situation safety behaviours in maintaining anxiety and negative beliefs. *Behavior Therapy*, *26*, 153–161.

Wells, A. & Morrison, T. (1994). Qualitative dimensions of normal worry and normal obsessions: a comparative study. *Behaviour Research and Therapy*, *32*, 867–870.

Wells, A. & Papageorgiou, C. (1998). Social phobia: effects of external attention on anxiety, negative beliefs and perspective taking. *Behavior Therapy*, *29*, 357–370.

Wells, A. & Papageorgiou, C. (2001). Social phobic interoception: effects of bodily information on anxiety, beliefs and self-processing. *Behaviour Research and Therapy*, *39*, 1–11.

Widiger, T. A., & Clark, L. A. (2000). Towards *DSM–V* and the classification of psychopathology. *Psychological Bulletin*, *126*, 946–963.

Williams, J. M. G. (1992). *The psychological treatment of depression: a guide to the theory and practice of cognitive behaviour therapy*. London: Routledge.

Williams, J. M. G. (1997). Depression. In D. M. Clark and C. G. Fairburn (Eds.), *Science and Practice of Cognitive Behaviour Therapy*. Oxford: Oxford University Press.

Williams, J. M. G. (2001). *Suicide and Attempted Suicide*. London: Penguin.

Williams, J. M. G., Mathews, A., & MacLeod, C. (1996). The emotional stroop task and psychopathology. *Psychological Bulletin, 120*, 3–24.

Wilson, G. T. (1996). Treatment of bulimia nervosa: when CBT fails. *Behaviour Research and Therapy, 34*, 197–212.

Wolfe, B. E., Metzger, E. D., Levine, J. M., Finkelstein, D. M., Cooper T. B., Jimerson, D. C. (2000). Serotonin function following remission from bulimia nervosa, *Neuropsycho-pharmacology. 22*, 257–263.

Wolpe, J. (1958). *Psychotherapy by Reciprocal Inhibition.* Stanford, CA: Stanford University Press.

Wolpe, J. (1961). The systematic desensitization treatment of neurosis. *Journal of Nervous Mental Disorders, 132*, 189–203.

Wolpe, J. (1962). Isolation of a conditioning procedure as the crucial psychotherapeutic factor: a case study. *Journal of Nervous Mental Disorders, 134*, 316–329.

Woody, S. R. & Rodriguez, B. F. (2000). Self-focused attention and social anxiety in socially anxious individuals and normal controls. *Cognitive Therapy and Research, 24(4)*, 473–488.

World Health Organisation (1992). *Tenth Revision of the International Classification of Diseases*. Geneva: WHO.

Yeragani, V. K., Rainey, J. M., Pohl, R., Balon, R., Berchou, R., Jolly, S., Lycaki, H. (1988). Preinfusion anxiety and laboratory-induced panic attacks in panic disorder patients. *Journal of Clinical Psychiatry, 49*, 302–306.

Yule, W., Udwin, O., & Murdoch, K. (1990). The 'Jupiter' sinking: effects in children's fears, depression and anxiety. *Journal of Child Psychology and Psychiatry, 31 (7)*, 1051–1061.

Index

absolutistic dichotomous thinking, 93
agoraphobia, 42, 43, 51
alprazolam, 51
American Psychiatric Association (APA), 14
   see also DSM-I; DSM-II; DSM-III; DSM-IV
amitriptyline, 96
amphetamine psychosis, 105
Anafranil, 71
anal stage, 20
anhedonia, 100
anorexia nervosa,
   biological factors in, 78
   cognitive behaviour therapy for, 83, 84
   cognitive model of, 79-81
   diagnosis of, 75
   differences from bulimia nervosa, 77
   drug therapy for, 81
antecedent events, 38
antidepressants, 51, 81, 84, 95, 96
anxiety disorders see generalised anxiety
   disorder (GAD); obsessive compulsive
   disorder (OCD)
anxiety management training (AMT), 53
apathy, 100
arbitrary inference, 92
asociality, 100
associative learning see classical
   conditioning
assumptions, in social phobia, 48
attentional bias, 25, 60, 69
attributes, 10
attribution, 94
atypical depression, 89
audio cued exposure, 72
autistic disorder, 102
autonomic nervous system (ANS), 45
avoidance behaviour, 33
avolition, 100

basal ganglia, 70
Beck, Aaron, 24-25, 91-93
behaviour therapy, 22, 23-24

see also cognitive behaviour therapy
behavioural characteristics, 10
behavioural experiments, 51-52, 72, 83, 97
behavioural family management (BFM),
   109-110
behavioural models,
   of obsessive compulsive disorder (OCD),
      68
   overview, 22-24
   see also learning theory
behavioural tests, 38
benzodiazepines, 51, 61, 62
binge-eating, 75
biological characteristics, 10
biological models,
   of depression, 94-95
   of eating disorders, 78
   of generalised anxiety disorder (GAD), 61
   of obsessive compulsive disorder (OCD),
      70-71
   overview, 26-28
biological therapy, 28
bipolar depression, 87, 88, 89
bipolar I disorder, 89
bipolar II disorder, 89
body image, 77, 80-81, 82-83
body mass index (BMI), 83, 84
borderline personality disorder, 17, 90
brain structure, 26-28, 70, 106-107
   see also neurotransmitters
bulimia nervosa,
   biological factors in, 78
   cognitive behaviour therapy for, 81-83,
      84
   diagnosis of, 76
   differences from anorexia nervosa, 77
   drug therapy for, 81, 84
Buspirone (Bu Spar), 62

Camberwell Family Interview (CFI), 104
catalepsy, 102
catastrophising, 59

catatonia, 100-101
catatonic depression, 90
catatonic immobility, 101
catatonic schizophrenia, 102
caudate nucleus, 70
causal attribution, 94
CBT *see* cognitive behaviour therapy
cerebellum, 27
characteristics, defining, 10
children *see* developmental psychology
chlorpromazine, 105, 109
citing references, 5
classical conditioning, 22-23, 33-34, 68
   see also conditioning
classification,
   method, 10-11, 12-13
   purpose of, 11-12
   see also DSM-I; DSM-II; DSM-III; DSM-IV
clomipramine, 71
cognitive behaviour therapy (CBT),
   for anorexia nervosa, 83, 84
   for bulimia nervosa, 81-83, 84
   for depression, 97, 98
   for generalised anxiety disorder (GAD),
     62, 62-63
   for obsessive compulsive disorder (OCD),
     72
   for panic disorder, 51-52, 53
   for schizophrenia, 109
   for social phobia, 52-53
   for specific phobias, 37
   see also cognitive therapy
cognitive behavioural group treatment
   (CBGT), 53
cognitive biases, 25, 37, 60-61, 92
cognitive characteristics, 10
cognitive dysmetria, 107
cognitive models,
   of anorexia nervosa, 79-81
   of depression, 91-93
   overview, 24-26
   of schizophrenia, 107-108
   of social phobia, 48-50, 52-53
   of specific phobias, 36-37
cognitive rehearsal, 97
cognitive restructuring, 51, 53, 82
cognitive therapy,
   for generalised anxiety disorder (GAD),
     55
   see also cognitive behaviour therapy
     (CBT)
collectively exclusive subclassification, 12
communication deviance, 104, 110

compulsions, 65, 67
computed axial tomography (CT scan), 106
concept, in classification, 12-13
conditioned response (CR), 23
conditioned stimulus (CS), 23
conditioning, 22-23, 33-34, 47, 79
   see also classical conditioning
conditions, in classification, 11, 12
conscious, the, 20
continuous disorders, 13
control, 69, 77, 80
cortex, frontal, 70
counter-conditioning, 24
critical thinking, 5
CT scan, 106
cultural biases, 16-17
cultural effects, 80
cyclothymic disorder, 89

Davey, Graham, 8
deadlines, 2
defining characteristics, 10
degradation, 26-27, 95
delusions,
   in depression, 90
   in schizophrenia, 100, 101
dementia praecox, 14
depression,
   alternative therapy for, 97
   cognitive behaviour therapy for, 97, 98
   cognitive model of, 91-93
   diagnosis of, 87-88, 90
   difficulty in diagnosing, 90
   drug therapy for, 96
   learned helplessness theory of, 93-94
   role of serotonin in, 94-95
   subtypes of, 88-90
developmental psychology, 20-21, 32-33
diagnosis, difficulties with, 16-17, 32, 43,
   57, 77, 88, 90
*Diagnostic and Statistical Manual of Mental
   Disorders see* DSM-I; DSM-II; DSM-III;
   DSM-IV
dichotomous thinking, 93
dieting, 82
discrete disorders, 13
disorganised schizophrenia, 100, 102
dopamine, 27, 95, 105, 109
double depression, 88
double-blind trials, 28
doxepin, 96
dream analysis, 21
drug therapy,

for depression, 96
for generalised anxiety disorder (GAD), 62
for panic disorder, 51
for schizophrenia, 109
for social phobia, 52
DSM-I (Diagnostic and Statistical Manual of Mental Disorders I), 14
DSM-II (Diagnostic and Statistical Manual of Mental Disorders II), 14
DSM-III (Diagnostic and Statistical Manual of Mental Disorders III), 14
DSM-IV (Diagnostic and Statistical Manual of Mental Disorders IV),
    anorexia nervosa in, 75
    axes of, 14-15
    bulimia nervosa in, 76
    criticisms against, 16-17
    depression in, 87-88
    generalised anxiety disorder (GAD) in, 55, 56
    obsessive compulsive disorder (OCD) in, 65-66
    panic diagnosis in, 42-43
    reliability of, 16
    revisions to, 14
    schizophrenia in, 101-103
    social phobia in, 44
    specific phobias in, 31-32
    validity of, 16
dysthymic disorder, 88, 89

eating disorders,
    biological factors in, 78
    learning role in, 79
    multicausality model of, 77-78
    overview, 74-75
    treatment of, 81-84
    see also anorexia nervosa; bulimia nervosa
echopraxia, 102
ECT (electro-convulsive therapy), 28
education, eating disorders and, 82
Effexor (venlafaxine), 96
ego, 21
Elavil (amitriptyline), 96
Electra complex, 20, 21
electro-convulsive therapy (ECT), 28
emotional stroop task, 25, 37, 60
essays, writing, 5
etiological validity, 16
evidence, in essays, 5, 6
evolution, specific phobias and, 36

examinations, university, 7-8
exercise, in bulimia nervosa, 76
expectancies, 34
exposure, 24, 37-38, 38-39, 53, 62, 71-72
exposure and response prevention (ERP), 71-72
expressed emotion, 104-105, 110

family therapy, 109-110
fasting, 76
fear, learned, 32-34
Fear Questionnaire, 38
Fear Survey Schedule, 38
fear-relevant stimuli, 35
fight-or-flight response, 44-45
Five Minute Speech Sample (FMSS), 104
flooding, 24, 39
fluoxetine, 71, 95, 96
free association, 20, 21
Freud, Sigmund, 20-22
frontal cortex, 70
functional magnetic resonance imaging (fMRI), 106, 107

gamma-aminobutyric acid (GABA), 61, 62
gender biases,
    in DSM, 16-17
    in psychodynamic theory, 21
general measure of adaptive functioning (GAFS), 14
generalised anxiety disorder (GAD),
    biological theories of, 61
    cognitive behaviour therapy for, 62, 62-63
    cognitive biases in, 60-61
    diagnosis of, 56-57
    drug therapy for, 62
    worry in, 57-60
genetics,
    role in schizophrenia, 103
    see also biological models
graded hierarchies, 24, 38, 39

hallucinations,
    in depression, 90
    in schizophrenia, 100, 101, 108
heterogeneity, 11-12
hierarchies, graded, 24, 38, 39
hippocampus, 27
Hippocrates, 14
homogeneity, 11-12, 18
homosexuality, 17
hormonal disorders, 28

hypervigilance, 47
hypnosis, 20
hypomania, 89
hypothalamus, 27, 94

ICD (International Classification of Disease), 14
id, 20
imagery, 8
imaginal exposure, 39
imipramine, 51, 53, 95, 96
inappropriate affect, 101
information-processing biases, 25
Interactional Communication Deviance, 104
International Classification of Disease (ICD), 14
isocaboxazid, 96
iterative thought process, 26

journals, 3-5

Kraepelin, Emil, 13-14

L-DOPA, 105
learned helplessness, 93-94
learning theory,
    of specific phobias, 32-34
    see also behavioural models;
        conditioning; preparedness theory
Legg, Charles, 7
Librium, 62
limbic system, 27, 45-46, 51, 94-95
'Little Albert', 33

magical thinking, 69
magnetic resonance imaging (MRI), 106
magnification, 92
maintenance factors, 38
major depressive disorder, 87
maladaptive thinking, 37
manic depression see bipolar depression
manic episodes, 88, 89
manic-depressive psychosis, 14
mapping, memory, 8
masochistic personality disorder, 17
measurement,
    in classification, 11
    of phobia severity, 38
medical student syndrome, 13
melancholic depression, 89
memory,
    as cognitive bias, 25
    in studying, 4-5, 8

mentalising, 107
meta-worry, 59-60
metarepresentation, 108
minimisation, 92-93
misinterpretation, 25, 60
mnemonics, 8
modelling, 34
monoamine oxidase inhibitors (MAOI), 96
monoamine theories of depression, 95
'mood-as-input' hypothesis, 59
mothering style, 103
motivation, 83
MRI (magnetic resonance imaging), 106
multicausality models, 78
mutism, 102
mutually exclusive subclassification, 12, 16

Nardil (phenelzine), 96
negative automatic thoughts (NATs), 91
negative cognitive triad, 92
negative symptoms, in schizophrenia, 100
negativism, 102
nerve impulse, 26, 27
nervous system, 26
neuroleptic drugs, 109
neurons, 26
neurotransmitters, 26, 27, 28, 45-46, 61
    see also dopamine; gamma-
        aminobutyric acid; norepinephrine;
        serotonin
neutralising, 72
non-associative theories, 35
non-purging type bulimia nervosa, 76
norepinephrine, 27, 45, 51, 78, 81, 95, 96
normalising, 71
normative fear, 32-33
note-taking, 3, 4-5
nucleus accumbens septi (NAS), 105

observational learning, 34
observer perspective, 49
obsessions, 58, 65, 66
obsessive compulsive disorder (OCD), 13
    behavioural explanations of, 68
    biological explanations of, 70-71
    cognitive theories of, 68-70
    descriptions of, 66-67
    diagnosis of, 65-66
    therapy for, 71-72
Oedipal complex, 20-21
oral stage, 20
outcome expectancies, 34
overgeneralisation, 92

panic disorder,
   biological theories of, 44-46
   cognitive behaviour therapy for, 51-52, 53
   cognitive model of, 46-47
   diagnosis of, 42-43
   drug therapy for, 51
   learning theories of, 47
paranoid schizophrenia, 102
parasympathetic nervous system, 45
parenting style, 103
Parnate (tranyleypromine), 96
paroxetine, 96
past papers, 7
Pavlov, Ivan, 23
Paxil (paroxetine), 96
penis envy, 21
perfectionism, 80
persecution, 100
perseveration, 26, 58, 59
personalisation, 93
pessimism, 92
phallic stage, 20
phenelzine, 96
phenothiazines, 105, 109
phobias see panic disorder; social phobia; specific phobias
physical characteristics, 10
placebo treatments, 28
political influence, in DSM, 17
positive symptoms, 100
post-event processing, 49, 50
post-mortems, 49, 50, 52-53
post-traumatic stress disorder, 17
postpartum depression, 90
pre-mortems, 48
predictive validity, 16, 21
preparedness theory, 35-36
problem-solving skills, 82
Prozac (fluoxetine), 71, 95, 96
psychoanalysis, 21-22
psychodynamic approaches, 19-22
psychosurgery, 28
psychotic depression, 90
punctuation, in essays, 7
purging, 75, 76

reality testing, 97
rebound effect, 58, 69
references, citing, 5
regional cerebral blood flow (rCBF), 106
rehearsal, cognitive, 97
relaxation therapy, 53, 62, 63

reliability, of DSM-IV, 16
research papers, 3
residual schizophrenia, 103
responsibility,
   in obsessive compulsive disorder (OCD), 69
   for own study, 1
restricting type anorexia nervosa, 75
reuptake, 26-27, 95
review papers, 3
revision, 7-8
rituals, 69
rumination, 26, 37, 53, 58, 59

sadistic personality disorder, 17
safety behaviours, 46, 49, 52
schizoaffective disorder, 102
schizophrenia,
   brain structure in, 106-107
   case studies, 101
   cognitive behaviour therapy for, 109
   cognitive theories of, 107-108
   diagnosis of, 101-103
   dopamine hypothesis of, 105, 109
   drug therapy for, 109
   family influences, 103-105
   family therapy for, 109-110
   genetic influences, 103
   social influences, 103-105
   symptoms of, 100-101
seasonal onset depression, 90
selective abstraction, 92
selective serotonin reuptake inhibitors (SSRIs), 95, 96
self-esteem, 80
self-monitoring, 82, 107, 108
self-processing, 49-50
Serax, 62
serotonin, 27, 51, 62, 70, 71, 78, 95
serotonin-norepinephrine reuptake inhibitors (SNRI), 96
Seroxat (paroxetine), 96
sertraline, 96
settings, 38
simple phobias see specific phobias
Sinequan (doxepin), 96
social anxiety disorder see social phobia
social influence, in schizophrenia, 103-105
social phobia,
   cognitive behaviour therapy for, 52-53
   cognitive model of, 48-50, 52-53
   diagnosis of, 43-44
   drug therapy for, 52

Socratic questioning, 83
somatic symptoms, in social phobia, 48, 50, 52
specific phobias,
    cognitive theories of, 36-37
    diagnosis of, 31-32
    learning theory of, 32-34
    non-associative theories of, 35
    preparedness theory of, 35-36
    therapy for, 37-39
specificity, in DSM, 16
spider phobia, 36
SSRIs (selective serotonin reuptake inhibitors), 95, 96
starvation, 80
stereotyped movements, 102
stigma, DSM and, 17
stroop task, 25, 37, 60
study skills, 1-5
subclassification, 12, 16
super-ego, 21
symbolism, 21
sympathetic nervous system, 45
synapses, 26
syndromes, 13
systematic desensitisation, 24, 39
systematic logical errors, 92-93
    see also cognitive biases

task assignment, 97
textbooks, 2-3, 4
thalamus, 27, 70
Thematic Apperception Tests, 104
thought catching, 97
thought suppression, 58, 69

thought-action fusion, 69, 71-72
time-management, 1-2, 8
token economies, 109
tranyleypromine, 96
trauma, and specific phobias, 33-34
tricyclic antidepressants (TCAs), 95, 96
triggers, 38, 46
twin studies, 103
two-factor theory of learned fear, 33-34, 68

unconditioned response (UCR), 23
unconditioned stimulus (UCS), 23
unconscious, the, 20
undifferentiated schizophrenia, 102
unipolar depression see major depressive disorder

validity, of DSM-IV, 16
Valium, 62
venlafaxine, 96
ventral tegmental area (VTA), 105
ventricles, 27, 28, 106
vicarious learning, 34

Watson, John, 22
waxy flexibility, 101, 102
weight, 77, 82, 83
willed action, 107, 108
Wisconsin Card Sort Test, 106
World Health Organisation, 14
worry, 57-60

Xanax, 51, 62

Zoloft (sertraline), 96